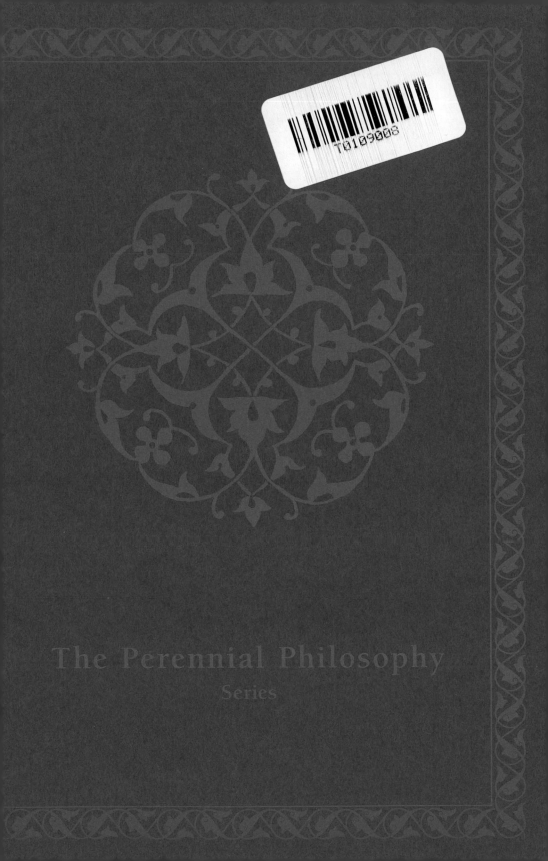

The Perennial Philosophy

Series

World Wisdom
The Library of Perennial Philosophy

The Library of Perennial Philosophy is dedicated to the exposition of the timeless Truth underlying the diverse religions. This Truth, often referred to as the *Sophia Perennis*—or Perennial Wisdom—finds its expression in the revealed Scriptures as well as the writings of the great sages and the artistic creations of the traditional worlds.

The Perennial Philosophy provides the intellectual principles capable of explaining both the formal contradictions and the transcendent unity of the great religions.

Ranging from the writings of the great sages who have expressed the *Sophia Perennis* in the past, to the perennialist authors of our time, each series of our Library has a different focus. As a whole, they express the inner unanimity, transforming radiance, and irreplaceable values of the great spiritual traditions.

Borderlands of the Spirit: Reflections on a Sacred Science of Mind appears as one of our selections in the Perennial Philosophy series.

The Perennial Philosophy Series

In the beginning of the Twentieth Century, a school of thought arose which has focused on the enunciation and explanation of the Perennial Philosophy. Deeply rooted in the sense of the sacred, the writings of its leading exponents establish an indispensable foundation for understanding the timeless Truth and spiritual practices which live in the heart of all religions. Some of these titles are companion volumes to the Treasures of the World's Religions series, which allows a comparison of the writings of the great sages of the past with the perennialist authors of our time.

Other Works by John Herlihy

♣

In Search of the Truth

The Seeker and the Way

Veils and Keys to Enlightenment

Modern Man at the Crossroads

Near and Distant Horizons

BORDERLANDS OF THE SPIRIT

♣

Reflections on a Sacred Science of Mind

by

John Herlihy

World Wisdom

Borderlands of the Spirit:
Reflections on a Sacred Science of Mind
© 2005 World Wisdom, Inc.

Library of Congress Cataloging-in-Publication Data

Herlihy, John.
  Borderlands of the spirit : reflections on a sacred science of mind /
by John Herlihy.
        p. cm. — (The Perennial philosophy series)
  Includes index.
  ISBN 0-941532-67-4 (pbk. : alk. paper)
  1. Faith and reason. 2. Knowledge, Theory of (Religion) I. Title.
II. Series.
  BL51.H472 2005
  202 — dc22

                                                        2004024954

Cover Art:
"Mist over the mountaintop"
by Sesson Shukei (c. 1504-1589)

Printed on acid-free paper in Canada

For information address World Wisdom, Inc.
P.O. Box 2682, Bloomington, Indiana 47402-2682

www.worldwisdom.com

♣

To my elder brother
Joseph Patrick Herlihy

Contents

And thou shalt love the Lord thy God with all thy heart,
and with all thy soul, and with all thy mind,
and with all thy strength.

Mark 12:30-31

♣

A mind that is stretched to a new idea
never returns to its original dimension.

Oliver Wendell Holmes

Preface

♣

Characteristics of the Borderland

We are primarily concerned in this endeavor with the possibility of spiritual experience during the modern era and the journey of discovery needed to lift the veil that divides the psyche of modern society from its other, its true self. The search for passageways to higher spiritual experience and the journey into the interior of the self commences where the world of science ends and the world of spirituality begins. Between these two worlds lies a borderland that serves as the defining isthmus separating these two paradigms of knowledge into two distinct realms of experience, each of which harbors unresolved questions and sets in motion critical consequences.

The traditional symbol of the isthmus dividing alien worlds recalls the symbolic image of the veil. In the Islamic context, the veil highlights the universal mystery at the center of existence, a mystery that serves as an invisible shield to protect the divine disclosure from undeserving and presumptuous eyes. Lifting such a veil reveals four stark images: a crossroads of decision and choice; the eye of the needle that serves as a rite of initiation into the world of ethics and morality; the sword bridge that crosses the great rift of the divided self; and the great sun door that leads into the interior, where human consciousness awakens the mind to introspection, where reflective thinking and sacred sentiment take root in the human heart, and where spiritual experience finds its true abode within the sacred ground of the soul.

The world of science and the world of spirituality exist as two separate and distinct worlds. The world of science represents the cognitive and rational world of the mind and the senses, while the world of spirituality denotes the intuitive and emotive worlds of the intellect and the heart. In more traditional times, they were distinct but interactive worlds that influenced each other to mutual benefit, and a person could move from one world to the other without taking notice of any hidden boundaries. In today's overwhelmingly secular environment, however, the two worlds of science and spirituality are alien worlds, distinguished primarily by a deep-seated antagonism in which the principles of spirituality and the pragmatism of modern science exist face to face in a perennial state of confrontation and challenge.

Between these two foreign countries lies an isthmus that separates them into two distinct polar realities and that serves as a no-man's land between two inviolate worlds, the one of human reason and the physical senses, the other of spiritual instinct and sacred intuition. Passing through this mediating provenance amounts to lifting the veil, opening the sun door, crossing the bridge over the abyss or passing through the eye of the needle as a rite of initiation into a world of knowledge and experience that would otherwise be inaccessible to the uninitiated. This isthmus, in memory of the isthmus that separates the two seas in the Quranic revelation, represents a borderland between alien worlds. We, as God's thinking creation, have the opportunity, by virtue of our innate human nature and the faculties of knowing and perception, to experience aspects of both worlds in such a manner that the knowledge of the outer world does not preclude the experience of the inner world, and that the knowledge of the inner world intensifies rather than dissipates the experience of the outer world.

Exploration of the borderland that links the external world of the reasoning mind, of the senses, and of the psychic ego with the inner world of spiritual instinct, sacred emotion, and higher consciousness is incumbent upon all human beings by virtue of the demands of their humanity, a "humanness" that implies above all an infusion of the vertical dimension of spirituality within the temporal and mundane setting of the purely physical and earthly experience. Within the isthmus, we can reflect the image of the world as well as the image of God. Insofar as we turn outward in dealing with the world, we become an image of the world; insofar as we turn inward and activate the higher faculties, we become an image of God and a reflection of His qualities and attributes.

We draw upon the image of the borderland as a domain of mediation and synthesis in order to emphasize the possibility that still exists for people today to cultivate an holistic experience of life that is based on the interaction of outer and inner worlds that ultimately come together as a synthesis in the unity of the one Reality. Our existential reality locks us in the embrace of an earthly duality that exists within the mind and psyche of the human being as the experience of the outer and inner worlds and that are aggrandized during these times within the two great worldviews of modern science and the traditional wisdom of the world religions. The supernal reality of the mind reveals an alternative topography that betokens the foreshadowing of some other world, some deeper life awaiting our attention that anticipates another kind of existence truer to our deepest yearning.

In this work, we intend to highlight the quest for a more complete understanding of the human experience by reflecting on the faculties of knowing and the fields of perception that characterize the borderland of which we write, including human reason, intelligence, heart knowledge, consciousness, spiritual imagination and sacred instinct, all of which are firmly embedded within the ground of the human soul and activated by a free will that can lead us out of ourselves and make transcendence of the human condition possible. The inner realm of the higher faculties constitutes a borderland and wilderness area that we need to more fully explore and experience if we ever wish to understand the universal mystery that underscores all existence. We must recognize this mystery as a fundamental truth of our existential reality if we are ever to achieve the knowledge of the true reality that all people, scientists included, unequivocally profess to be the ultimate goal of the modern, thinking individual.

One cannot help but have a feeling of entering the environs of a "lost world" when considering the characteristics of this borderland. The traditional world of the spirit has become a phantom from a remote past that is nearly unrecognizable in today's world except as a distant specter of a world now passed by. The faculty of the human intellect that was once capable of the direct perception of the Divinity no longer exists as a viable option for modern humanity. This open door to the Infinite seems to have been irrevocably closed to the contemporary modern mindset. The mind now relies solely on the perception of an externalized intelligence on the one hand, and a creative and fertile imagination on the other, to help navigate the way through the mysteries and challenges that confront people in today's modern world. The brave, the sensitive, the intelligent and open heart of yore—what we call in this work "the other heart, the forgotten one"—is only a vague sentiment of its former self, a heart that once took root in the ground of the soul and could see reflected in the promise of some future world the primordial beginning of time.

One point worth mentioning as we commence this endeavor is the fact that the human being does not, and never will perceive the reality directly, at least not within this world. Behind all the theories of modern science and the perennial message of the spiritual traditions lies the realization that humanity will not see the Face of God and will only perceive the Reality "through a glass darkly" (1 Corinthians 13:12) or from behind a veil. Particle physics and molecular biology clearly highlight this truth by forcing scientists to observe the subatomic world of quantum mechanics through highly sophisticated devices rather than the naked eye, in order to witness the activity of the sub-atomic world of protons and electrons by suggestion as it were. The traditions highlight this truth by requiring the faithful to perceive the true nature of Reality indirectly through the words of revelation, through signs and symbols within the world of nature, and through the inner experience that characterizes the borderlands of the spirit that still exist within the lost continent of the inner being.

♣ ♣ ♣

In its overall design, this work consists of three distinct parts. Part One is concerned with the primary faculties of knowing, including the direct and spontaneous knowledge obtained through the intellect, the analysis of knowledge through the faculty of reason, the synthesis of knowledge through human intelligence, and a heart knowledge that unites the knowledge of God with human sentiments and higher emotions. Part Two deals with the broad field of human perception as it is experienced through the prism of spiritual imagination, sacred sentiments and the insights of the soul. Part Three reflects upon the rarefied "energy" generated by the higher faculties that expresses itself as a force field of spirituality within the life of a person. To that end, we portray human faith as a beacon of light within the shadowlands of the modern world, explore the paradox of free will as a potent force in confronting the inescapable choices that life offers us, and, finally, highlight the significance of human language in communicating the richness of a person's inner life to the outside world.

According to the projected worldview of empirical science, the modern prototype human being does not have a soul, a definable human nature, a heart that thinks, an intellect that knows intuitively, sentiments that are inspired, or an enlightened human consciousness. The initial spark and perennial afterglow of these higher faculties still lie outside the understanding of modern science. As essential human faculties and modes of perception, they are understood to be fundamental in identifying who we are within the traditional religious worldview. The faculties and force fields of intuition, heart sentiment, emotion, instinct, and imagination that connect us to one another, that are the basis of all our higher knowledge and emotions, and that are beyond anything our words can say but which articulate the way the heart is—are all these lost from the new, scientific identity of the modern, prototype human being? The answer, of course, must be a definitive no, unless we as modern individuals wish to cut ourselves off from the roots of our human meaning and the very source of our true origin.

If there was ever a reality that could make itself known, where intimacy could be experienced, where higher knowledge could be actualized, where consciousness could radiate as a living presence, where spiritual imagination and sacred instinct could unite with formal worship to build an inner life with value and meaning, if such a reality truly exists, it will make itself known and felt within the borderlands of the spirit. Within this frontier lies the no-man's land between outer and inner worlds, a sacred precinct where the Divinity is remembered, where human beings do not forget themselves, and where they are not forgotten in return, close upon the void where the assumptions of modern science end and the mani festations of God's prerogative begin.

This rarefied landscape consists of two borders, the one leading back into the world of nature, of humanity and the earth, where the duality of the life experience is encountered and where a sense of the relative, the subjective and the contingent prevails; the other leading inward into the world of the spirit where human transcendence serves as the motivating goal and a knowledge of the Objective, the Absolute, and the Transcendent prevails as the final destination of the spiritual path. Within the realm of the borderland we are able to see—when the time is right and the conditions for exposure have been met—at an inverted angle, akin to the sixth sense of animals or the revered third eye, allowing us to perceive a knowledge that is enlightening and to experience a world that is miraculous.

Let us leave behind the split-gate of this world and the split-image of humanity, both of which highlight the duality of this world, and pass through the great sun door into the interior of the self. Those who wish to accompany me in this endeavor need not look for the framework of a formal world religion because it is not my intention within this work to project a prescribed pathway; but rather to characterize and come to terms with the human faculties that form the bridge between two alien worlds and to explore the fields of perception that lead to unexpected spiritual consequences. No one religion has exclusive rights over the human soul. People see and understand things differently, and I can report only from the region of my own spiritual wilderness what I see of God's signs and wonders.

It is important to realize that everyone possesses such a wilderness area whose entry creates a feeling of unbounded liberation and immense uncharted distances. Within this frontier a person can roam indefinitely, where no physical objects will clutter the open range of the imagination and where time goes by as in a dream with no real validity or meaning. You are entering the inner kingdom of the spirit, where the knowledge of God awaits the mindfulness of human consciousness and the desire to cross the sword bridge between the human and Divine Reality could lead ultimately to the final illumination.

Part One

♣

Faculties of Knowledge

Chapter One

♣

Reason Wears a Wizard's Cap

The eye by which I see God is the same as the eye by which God sees me.
My eye and God's eye are one and the same.
   (Meister Eckhart)

A fool sees not the same tree that a wise man sees.
   (William Blake)

We commence our endeavor of examining the faculties of knowing and perception by making an initial reference to the unique phenomenon of the modern mentality: its instinctive reliance on human reason to negotiate its way through the mystery that lies at the heart of human existence. Underlying the entire scientific premise is this presumption that human reason is somehow guaranteed access to the profound truths of the universe on its own terms. Needless to say, this assertion begs the question: are we as modern[1] individuals supposed to settle for a secular—as opposed to a sacred—science that has no credible answer to the perennial mysteries that surround us? Are we to accept without question the aura of truth and finality that colors the speculative pronouncements of modern science concerning the true nature of ultimate reality?

Is there, indeed, no decisive Truth that transcends all human speculation, a truth that could overwhelm us with its veracity and its certitude? Is it not possible that at the heart of the universal mysteries we seek to comprehend there lies a seed waiting to evolve into a paradigm of knowledge whose manifestation and growth will resolve the perennial questions with a certainty that continues to elude the findings of modern science, even though science's empirical system of belief and secular philosophy now

---

1. This term will be clarified further on in the chapter; for now it will suffice to understand the term modern as referring to those who have come this far and have profited from the knowledge and experience of generations since time immemorial and who are now on the verge of a new, dynamic future of unknown proportion.

play such a vital role in shaping the attitude and ambiance of the human condition?

We live in the divided house of the modern mind which extols a reductionist approach to the understanding of the body, mind, and heart, rather than the unified vision of the One Reality which brings these modes of being together in a sacred interaction of holy faith and human reason. With the rise of modern science, faith's luster has gradually lost its sheen and reason has come to be understood as the only true standard through which the basis of all knowledge could be established. Through the light of reason, the 20th century mentality finally gained complete access to all knowledge based on the model of inquiry and experimentation of the natural sciences. Having passed through the cold logic of human reasoning, knowledge is now to be considered factual, deductive and empirical, based on the universal laws of mathematics and the physical presence of matter, whose self-evident objectivity cannot be denied.

Throughout the modern era, in spite of the efforts of contemporary scientists to satisfy the fundamental mysteries that haunt the human psyche, the pursuit of scientific knowledge has left modern humanity feeling edgy and put upon. We no longer question what we know and helplessly accept the expert notions of the scientific community.[2] We assume the validity of what we know and want possibly to know more, but without asking the vital question: How do we know what we know? The fault lies undoubtedly in the question. We no longer question what we know. Indeed the certainty of our assumptions leaves no room to alter or compromise our assertions about the true nature of the reality. What remains of the cosmic mystery merely awaits our scrutiny and resolution.

Faith and reason need not be the mortal enemies of the self, however, creating a psychic fault line through the inner landscape of our cognitive world. Instead they could be understood as complements with the power to reunite body with soul, reason with intellect, matter with spirit in order to bridge the great rift that separates the sacred and profane worlds. Faith's intuitive light understands

---

2. A case in point, for example, is the theory of evolution. Try telling the average person, much less a scientist, that evolution is still an unproved theory and you'll be taken for a madman, if not a fool. It is as if to suggest that a possible chink exists in the armor of this sacrosanct belief would bring their world (view) crashing down around them.

everything within nature and humanity to be a transcendent symbol of a higher reality that casts rays of the sacred across every aspect of our earthly life. Human reason need not be the cold, autonomous standard of mind that we make it out to be, replacing the intellect as the sovereign instrument of visionary knowledge and insight. After all, what actually prevents reason from being a door of perception that leads us out of ourselves and makes everything appear as it truly is—a symbolic image of the infinite and the eternal—except perhaps reason itself?

Within the interior of the human world we find distinctive characteristics that distinguish humans as unique among all living things. These features include higher order faculties such as discursive reasoning, visionary intelligence, a broad range of emotions, moral sensibility, and an intuitive sense of the sacred and the otherworldly. Although in some cases appearances might indicate otherwise,[3] we are so far removed from the cognitive levels of the animal kingdom that we simply cannot account for ourselves on the basis of purely natural processes within the existing laws of nature. On both rational and symbolic levels, human reason and the natural order itself actually call out and yearn for the spirit of a transcendent intelligence that we feel within our very bones and that we witness in the complexity and design of the universe from the double helix of DNA to the magisterial procession of the galaxies. Both human reason and its natural complement, intelligence, find their venue for self-directed mental activity within the borderland of the spirit which constitutes a kind of sacred precinct of our inner being that relies on the higher faculties that actually have no dependence on the externalized physical world.

♣ ♣ ♣

We shall make repeated reference to the term *modern* and its derivations throughout the course of this book; it would therefore be wise to give an account of its meaning at the outset so as to avoid any unnecessary confusion of terms. By the word *modern* we do not wish to suggest a reference to a specific temporality as such, to

3. A certain similarity between the simian and human worlds and the nearly identical chromosomal count between chimps and man certainly qualify as analogous possibilities.

highlight the new, for example, as opposed to the old; nor do we mean a condition of knowing about things that were not known in earlier times and whose mystique therefore takes on the flavor of a development to which earlier generations merely gave crude expression. Architecture and technology, for example, are now perceived to be a reflection of modern culture versus the archaic or old-fashioned structures of former times and the temperaments that built them.

The word *modern* in the context of this work relies on the qualifying terms scientific, secular, and rational to substantiate its meaning and highlight its particular focus. The term *modern* and its counterpart *modernity* have evolved over time into a meaning that fully summarizes the ambiance and point of view of the rational, secular and scientific spirit of inquiry that colors and shapes the very mentality of the age in which we live. When we refer to modern humanity, the modern mentality, and modern science throughout this work, we mean none other than the rational, secular, scientific and increasingly scientistic[4] outlook that prevails worldwide and that characterizes the prevailing worldview of the modern era.

The modern mentality, and the modern worldview that is the product of that mentality, for all its sheer innovativeness, its technical brilliance, its formidable modes of intelligence and perception, its practical applications, and its sophisticated assertions of a credible worldview, has backed itself into a corner in which there is not much room to maneuver and from which there is little hope of escape. It could be symbolically represented as the closed system of the mind's "I" that bases its first principles on purely hypothetical conjecture and speculative theory on the one hand, and a series of categorical denials on the other; rather than the open door of the mind's "eye" that bases its intuition and resulting faith on the principle of a first cause and a final end as

---

4. "There is a sharp yet oft-overlooked distinction between scientific knowledge and scientistic belief. And the difference is simple: authentic knowledge of a scientific kind refers necessarily to things that are observable in some specified sense, and affirms a verifiable truth; scientistic belief, on the other hand, is distinguished precisely by the absence of these positivistic attributes. Thus, no matter what may be its 'scientific status,' the latter refers to entities that are not in truth observable, and affirms something that is in fact unverifiable" (Wolfgang Smith, *Cosmos & Transcendence* [Peru, Ill: Sherwood Sugden & Company, 1984], p. 9).

the ultimate Source of the universe and its principal defining quality.

Modern science strives to reduce the whole of the qualitative richness of the universe to a purely quantitative mathematical formula. As such, it boldly casts aside the so-called vertical perspective portrayed within the great spiritual traditions, which perceive an inner dimension to every external form, an enduring spirit behind the temporality of matter, and an abiding truth with the power to synthesize every physical fact into a union of meaning and purpose. In so doing, modern science effectively closes the open door to the Infinite and denies humanity any possibility of fulfilling its true vocation on earth as a physical form animated by the breath and spirit of God, a thinking and conscious being created by God and cast into a physical and human form.

In spite of the aura of objectivity, certainty, and invincibility set forth by the contemporary scientific establishment, the modern scientific endeavor and the high priests of science who religiously uphold its doctrines, have a lot to account for.[5] The modern scientific outlook and its approach to the pursuit of knowledge initially entertains theories and suppositions that must ultimately be supported by a body of empirical evidence that is believed to lend an aura of objectivity and a quality of the absolute to its procession of speculative thinking. Although this approach may pose as an intriguing and legitimate endeavor, it still begs the question: What substantiates the truth of a fully reasoned but unproved hypothesis, and what objectifies the reality of the physicality of a transient and temporal matter, that they have the power to substantiate and objectify the true nature of ultimate reality?

Moreover, the modern scientific approach to the pursuit of knowledge harbors a misguided and questionable faith in the absolute veracity of its first principles, namely its unchallenged assumption that the laws of mathematics provide the categorical

---

5. Ironically, scientists often resort to religious terminology to clarify their points, making reference for example to the "canonical definition of objective scientific knowledge" and the "grail of objective truth." The Harvard professor and biologist E. O. Wilson goes well beyond the decorum of professional neutrality when, with reference to the objective truth of modern science, he writes, ". . . Ignorance-based metaphysics will back away step by step, like a vampire before the lifted cross" (*Consilience* [New York: Vintage, 1999], p. 68).

imperative of the human mind in the formation of all scientific theory. Perhaps they do and perhaps they do not. Who or what has the right to decide whether the laws of mathematics should determine what is real and what is unreal in the natural and supernatural order? Is the knowledge entertained by the faculty of reason the result of its function within a purely human and rational order, or from a supra-individual and metaphysical order? The same question keeps recurring in many different guises: What will provide the ultimate criterion for a knowledge that will be not only scientific but also universal, an objective knowledge that will transcend the limitations of the natural world and the human condition? The quest for a unified theory of knowledge is what everyone wants to know and it drives many of the leading proponents of modern science to the far ends of the earth to uncover.

Finally, the modern scientific outlook continues to remain uncomfortable with the prototype image it has created. It steadfastly maintains an attitude of awkward ambivalence toward the full capabilities of the human persona in terms of the intelligence, the range and extent of human reasoning, and human consciousness as an afterthought of a mindless evolutionary process that traces its line of origin back to some form of animal ancestry. The still mysterious and incredible theory of evolution, when applied to the development of the cognitive, discerning, and reflective mind, only heightens the mystery surrounding the origin of human vs. animal intelligence, the higher faculties and fields of perception, and the meaning and import of our true humanity. In other words, the modern frame of reference and the scientific worldview we now live in do not admit of the borderland of the spirit of which we write. The modern mentality does not fully appreciate the richness and fullness of the human faculties of intelligence, the reasoning powers of the mind, higher consciousness, the fields of perception, spiritual imagination, sacred emotions and ultimately the meaning of the soul in the same way that these higher faculties were understood during more traditional times, namely as basically human properties capable of transcendence: human by virtue of the human condition and transcendent by virtue of the human image as a reflection of a divine Principle.

Modern science and the predominant worldview that provides the framework for its findings is mind and matter bound. It is fixated on the ability of reason to work its way through any dilemma and the need for empirical evidence to quantify and fully objectify its theories. Moreover, the modern mentality permits itself the luxury of a dream in which the faculty of reason is somehow transcendent, that is to say, a faculty that has the power to surpass itself beyond its natural capabilities *by its own means*; a faculty that in pursuit of its self-ordained inquiry into the true nature of reality will ultimately unearth sufficient evidence to substantiate the miracle of existence *on its own*.

The modern-day reliance on the determining powers of human beings and the absolute trust in the ability of human reason to lead us into the future of ourselves, on our own and without the aid of Heaven, tends to dominate the first tier of our inner world with its superficial line of reasoning and its closed system of thought. The mind, with its intricate thought processes, moves from the phenomenal world of the senses to the inner world of thought and abstraction and back out again into the world of created forms with an assurance that is frankly astounding and that belies the truly mysterious nature of our inner world. The question, however, lingers at the edge of consciousness: What lies beyond the first tier of the mind?

No one doubts that the faculty of reason plays a vital role in the inner discourse of the mind; but the reality of our inner life—at both conscious and unconscious levels—goes far beyond what the faculty of reason can account for. There is something happening within the human mind that leads us far beyond the literal and logical proceedings of our rational mind. Like "the wind that bloweth where it listeth" (John 3:8), our minds move in uncertain and unpredictable ways. Our imagination portrays possibilities that lead us beyond the apparent self; our understanding arises from a dimension for which we cannot fully account. Ultimately, we arrive at thoughts, ideas, and resolutions that have their own mysterious origin and that offer no explanation beyond their ability to enlighten the mind, raise our consciousness, and offer the certainty for which the human heart yearns.

What, then, are we as modern individuals to make of the faculty of human reason? What should it accomplish for modern humanity, and how and why? Does it establish the *raison d'être* of the human being? Does it define human meaning according to the proclamations of the scientific paradigm of knowledge? Does it actually permit human beings to maneuver through the corridors of the mind in a way that allows them to transcend the limitations of a matter-based mind? If so, what is the ultimate source of such explanatory power and such potential illumination? Does today's faculty of reason observe, witness, and exercise awareness in the same way that the intellect and higher consciousness of the people living in an earlier, more traditional culture functioned, drawing as they did on the source material of revelation and the capacity of the higher faculties to recognize and appreciate the direct knowledge of God? Is the modern concept of reason actually the mind's "I," the psychologized ego of the 21st century personality that serves as a pale reflection of the mind's "eye" of the religions, the "eye of certainty" referred to in the Quranic revelation, the third eye that reflects a higher dimension, or the eye of Shiva that is symbolic of the gift of spiritual vision?

According to the prevailing scientific worldview, the only possible answer must be a resounding no, for nothing and no one today wants to play the shadow figure and be the dark afterthought to an illuminated faculty or first principle. The realm of the shadowland must traditionally be considered the domain of unreality and illusion, where a pale horse and rider pose as the real thing, when in truth they are merely phantom shadows representing the unrealities they truly are. To rely on reason alone as the mechanism to process human thoughts in a manner that reflects the whole person is to live in the shadowlands of the lower self and to rely on a faculty of mind that was originally intended—but no longer serves—as a bridge to the higher faculties and modes of perception.

In other words, human reason was not intended to be a one-horse rider serving the impressions of the human senses and directing them through the filter of the human ego, for this in fact only represents the first tier of humanity's inner world. According to the traditional Islamic perspective, human reason (*al-aql*) serves as a bridge between the lower world of the mind-body relationship and the higher world of the intellect-spirit relationship; it thus takes an active part in the borderland of the spirit as a human faculty illuminated by the superior realms of the intellect and not the shadow self that it has become in today's rational and scientistic environment.

Perhaps we need to understand the traditional concept of the faculty of reason from a different angle of approach. According to traditional philosophy, we live within the rhythms of the earth and enjoy an easy familiarity with the harmony those rhythms convey. The enduring cycles of nature are reflected in the changing seasons in the life of humans. The waxing of spring becomes the waning of winter, just as the expansion of childhood and youth matures into middle age and maturity, only to diminish again in old age and finally senescence. The seasons and cycles of nature and earthly life seem to interact in ways that suggest a broad complementarity of purpose and design between the rhythms of human beings and nature.

So much for appearances; and yet the truth of the cosmos would be impossible to conjure if it were not more than what it appears to be. Within the harmony of the natural cosmic order lies a dark and sobering symbolic message. Everyone is familiar with the two faces of the earth. The sun casts down its light to give us the face of day, while the rotation of the earth turns us away from the sun to give us the face of night. The mystery of day and night is unceremoniously resolved in the relative fixity of the sun and the rhythmic fluidity of our planet Earth as it floats on its orbit. The message is self-evident to the casual observer, or do appearances again mislead? Is there contained within the darkness of night a lingering secret that refuses to shed its moon glow of light?

In fact, the cosmic Eye has a different perspective than the human one. The sun casts down its light upon the earth in the form of an ever-expanding ray, while the earth sends forth its night back out into the cosmos in an ever-receding shadow coming to a point at the wall of infinity. The earth's day wears its pale luminescence like a mantle of blue, while the earth's night wears its conical shadow like a wizard's cap.[6]

In this way, we arrive at a conception of reason that transcends the narrow and limited framework of the scientific perspective, which invests much of its identity in the ability of matter to objectify reality. The immense intelligence displayed in nature and the timeless rhythms of the natural order are reflected as similar properties within the human mind, most notably in the instrument of human reason whose cognitive rationalism can react with interest to the

6. The image of the wizard's cap is drawn from Chet Raymo's *The Soul of the Night: An Astronomical Pilgrimage* (Saint Paul, Minnesota: Hungry Mind Press, 1992).

intuitive insights and natural rhythms of a higher order. If we are not careful in the way we express our modernity, we may end up wearing the wizard's cap, sending shadows in every direction when we should be reflecting the influences of a supra-rational luminescence.

Every object in the vicinity of an illuminating sun carries with it a cone of night whose shadow-draped stylus casts its signature into the surrounding void. Why should human nature be any different, if not the very antithesis of natural law? Human beings and their higher faculties of mind are no exception; they are the example *prima facie* of the universal norm, whether they walk across the earth in search of livelihood and fulfillment or traverse the borderlands of some inner universe. They can always count on the light of intelligent intuition to shine across the surface of their being, just as a person's physical form always casts a shadow.

In the next chapter, we will write more extensively about the luminosity of the human intellect as a direct reflection of the Supreme Intellect, by virtue of whose reflection we as human beings are able to transcend the limitations of the earthly realm and reunite once again with the presence of a Supreme Being. Perhaps it is no small miracle then that as rational beings, we have the use of the faculty of reason with which to traverse the inner landscape of thought and reflection in a logical and ordered manner. Like the conical darkness of the night that leaves its mark on the universal void, the stylus of our inner being can engrave its signature and leave its mark on the mystery of the individual self. Whether we use our faculty of reason as an instrument of light or darkness remains a decision that is ours alone to make, a decision that will determine the true nature of our unfolding destiny.

♣ ♣ ♣

Two predominant trends exist within contemporary thinking concerning the true nature of human intelligence. Firstly, we need to reckon with the uncompromising dogma of reductionism, the methodology of choice among the scientific community in search of a unified knowledge that can explain virtually everything. Secondly, and by way of complement, we need to come to terms with the progressive research into identifying the neural activity of the brain as the sole source of intelligent mind and human consciousness.

Reductionism tries to comprehend one level of scientific phenomena in terms of concepts and processes that occur at a lower and more fundamental level of existence. In chemistry, for example, large-scale reactions are accounted for by examining the behavior of molecules. Physiologists study the activity of living cells in terms of processes carried out by organelles and other sub-cellular entities. The predilection of modern scientists to approach the understanding of the phenomenal world in purely reductionist terms attempts to limit the intelligence to the strictly human frame of reference, namely brain matter, human reasoning, and the insights of the physical senses.

Francis Crick and Philip Anderson are two scientists who represent the bookends of the broad spectrum of the reductionist argument. Francis Crick, a noted physicist and biochemist who collaborated with James D. Watson in the discovery of the molecular structure of DNA, has expressed in no unspoken terms the ultimate reductionist statement in the very first sentence of his book *The Astonishing Hypothesis*: "You, your joys and your sorrows, your memories and your ambitions, your sense of personal identity and free will, are in fact no more than the behavior of a vast assembly of nerve cells and their associated molecules. As Lewis Carroll's Alice might have phrased it, 'You're nothing but a pack of neurons.'"[7] Philip Anderson, on the other hand, who won the Nobel Prize in 1977, has echoed the traditional spirit, which contends that there are hierarchical levels of reality in some sense independent of, rather than dependent on, each other. "At each stage, entirely new laws, concepts, and generalizations are necessary, requiring inspiration and creativity to just as great a degree as in the previous one. Psychology is not applied biology, nor is biology applied chemistry."[8]

7. Francis Crick, *The Astonishing Hypothesis* (New York: Simon & Schuster, 1994), p. 3. This is an astonishing contention that actually constitutes the astonishing hypothesis of Crick's title.

8. John Horgan, *The Undiscovered Mind: How the Human Brain Defies Replication, Medication, and Explanation* (New York, Simon & Schuster, 1999), pp. 258-259. Evolutionists do not refer to the hierarchical order of nature. According to Seyyed Hossein Nasr: "They reduced mind to the result of evolutionary development—that is, purely material processes—that moved toward every greater organization, resulting finally in human life and consciousness. The reductionism of modern science thereby took a giant step by reducing the other half of Cartesian dualism to matter and ending with a monistic materialism that characterizes so much of modern biology. . . ." (*Religion and the Order of Nature* [Oxford: Oxford University Press, 1996], pp. 145-146).

Reason is the cognitive faculty considered by the scientific establishment to be decisive in establishing the criteria that leads to the formulation of scientific knowledge. It can be summarized as humanity's capacity to reason its way through the labyrinth of scientific knowledge. Scientists hope to arrive at an understanding of the true nature of reality through the human ability to objectify existence within the physical and natural order through the objectifying power of the physical senses and the explanatory power in the reasoning of the human mind. Thinkers who would attribute to the mind nothing more than an epiphenomenal capacity suggest that this thinking process, far from echoing higher, supra-rational modes of awareness, is based on the belief that what we come to know is the input and the product of our physical senses and is ultimately attributed to cellular activity and genetic inheritance. In some kind of exclusive manner, our ideas must be applicable to the phenomenal world that is disclosed to us through the physical evidence and quantified with exactitude to the nth degree through the laws of mathematics.

Our sense experience constitutes more valuable evidence in support of the hypotheses of modern science than the other modes of conscious experience available to us, such as the intuitions and insights of the imagination and the higher emotions. Of course, everyone knows that the senses cannot be fully trusted[9] and that it is therefore not so much the senses themselves but the laws and principles of mathematics inherent in what the senses can measure that really count and that form the final criteria of objectivity. Only what can be expressed in mathematical terms can ultimately be identified as a reality within nature. Anything that cannot be explained in physical terms through empirical evidence and framed within the context of a mathematical law is summarily reduced to the domain of the subjective. No other comment could be more pejorative and suspect in today's climate of opinion than that something is only a psychological,[10] and therefore subjective, mode of manifestation.

9. Look at what the eye perceives with regard to the activity of the sun, moon and stars; indeed look at what the human eye does with the quantum world that it cannot even perceive on its own.
10. Perhaps it is further symptomatic of today's intellectual climate of opinion that much of the traditional terminology has become "inverted." Thus, the word "myth," which was originally intended to suggest or recall a "reality," now connotes an "untruth," whereas the traditional science of man's inner psychology was at one time very much "real" insofar as it dealt with and reflected a "science" of the human soul.

Secondly, the modern individual, by following in the footsteps of the leading world scientists, fervently maintains a predisposition—perhaps one should call it by its rightful name of prejudice—to conceive of intelligence as nothing more than the intelligent reflection of organized matter based on the neural activity of the brain, although why such a conception should be appealing to the human mind is anyone's guess.[11] The well-known writer and astronomer, the late Carl Sagan, wrote in his book *Dragons of Eden*: "My fundamental premise about the brain is that its workings—what we sometimes call 'mind'—are a consequence of its anatomy and physiology and nothing more."[12] This is a fairly definitive statement on a subject highly qualified by the suspect nature of its pure speculation. Once again, we quote Francis Crick, the biologist who has gone where no one else has gone before. Writing in his book *Of Molecules and Men* on the subject of whether biology needs to be explained in terms of life forces lying outside the domain of physics, he asserts: "The ultimate aim of the modern movement in biology is in fact to explain *all biology* in terms of physics and chemistry."[13] Perhaps we need not look for a more characteristic example of the reductionist spirit than in the radical "*all biology*" of this statement (italics mine).

In another corner of the scientific universe, neuroscientists have been trying to close the gap between the brain and the mind. Many neuroscientists now believe that all aspects of the mind, including its most puzzling attribute—human consciousness and its implicit self-awareness—are likely to be explainable in a more materialistic way as the behavior of large sets of interacting neurons. Some even believe that consciousness arises from quantum-physical processes taking place in microtubules, which are protein structures inside neurons. They are busy attempting to show that consciousness is simply "an emergent property" (whatever that means) arising from brain cells, whose behavior can be explained with the actions of chemistry, the organization of molecules, and the behavior of

11. Things like intelligence, intellectual intuition, and the higher emotions—indeed the very higher faculties of the mind—need to be reduced to a matter-based, provable, and thus objective, doctrine according to the party line of the scientific establishment. Anything that undermines that doctrine undermines the very foundation upon which the establishment is built.
12. Carl Sagan, *The Dragons of Eden* (New York: Ballantine Books, 1977), p. 7.
13. Francis Crick, *Of Molecules and Men* (Seattle: University of Washington Press, 1966), p. 10.

atoms. The powers of the mind in this instance arise (or emerge) from the physical laws affecting brain matter.[14] According to this ultra-reductionist view of the mind, the brain is everything while the mind is actually a linguistic formality that serves a useful purpose by allowing communication through a medium that is actually only the nominal sum of its parts and has no reality of its own. Psychic and spiritual life, not to mention the vagaries of human emotion, are understood to be epiphenomena of brain functions and nothing more.

Not all scientists hold this view and the debate will undoubtedly continue for quite some time. An increasing number of brain experts have come to believe that the purely materialist position is unrealistic and that the phenomena of perception can only be explained through an equally real—and vital—second element, namely mind. "Because it seems to be certain that it will always be quite impossible to explain the mind on the basis of neuronal action within the brain, and because it seems to me that the mind develops and matures independently throughout an individual's life as though it were a continuing element, and because a computer (which the brain is) must be operated by an agency capable of independent understanding, I am forced to choose the proposition that our being is to be explained on the basis of two fundamental elements."[15] This statement seems as honest as it is brave, considering the rigid opposition to any hint of activity independent of the physical world that may impinge upon the foundations of the scientific worldview.

Scientists hope that this reductionist hypothesis of the mind will lead to an explanation of how the brain makes decisions or even how it proves mathematical theorems. Even if it gets that far, however, the theory is still silent about how these processes give rise to conscious experience. Indeed the same problem arises with any

14. Antonio R. Damasio, in a special Winter Issue 1998 of *Time*, has added an intriguing afterthought to the argument in his article "A Clear Consciousness": "And yet something else may be needed—not some divine spark or soul, but some as yet unknown aspect of brain activity." Indeed, something "unknown" must be at work, yet why should it necessarily be an aspect of "brain activity" and not merely a mystery suggesting another dimension of reality altogether?
15. Wilder Penfield, *The Mystery of the Mind* (Princeton: Princeton University Press, 1975), quoted by E. F. Schumacher in his *A Guide for the Perplexed* (New York: Harper & Row, 1977), p. 76.

theory of consciousness based on purely physical processing alone. This must lead us to the observation that if the human mind were merely the reflection of organized matter, and although this may be the contemporary idea of intelligence, it is certainly not the kind of intelligence envisioned by the traditional sages who believed human intelligence to participate in a transcendent principle reflected within the human being as an individualized beacon of light drawn from an otherworldly, supra-individual source.

For now, modern science endorses the idea that humanity has the power to fully rationalize the thinking process, while the concept of humanism, which is the logical by-product of the rational mind, reduces everything to the merely human. To that end, the faculty of reason[16] has assumed the mantle of the highest human function, which, together with the observation of the senses, has led to the birth of the scientific methodology and the philosophy of contemporary rationalism. Rationalism elevates human reason to the level of principal faculty within the human being; reason processes incoming knowledge and serves as the final criterion for judging the objectivity and truth of anything and everything. The faculties of imagination, emotion, sentiment, the cognitive abilities, and especially the sphere of the senses, are all under the influence and control of the faculty of reason to provide the framework and balance for the workings of the mind, whose ultimate purpose is to discover a unified theory of knowledge that will identify the true nature of the cosmic reality, in keeping with the parameters established by none other than human reason.

Instead of human reason being a practical instrument that is complementary to an authentic human intelligence as the religious traditions suggest, modern science portrays this noble faculty as the objective pole of a qualifying reality and the very axis of human intelligence. It thereby provides the ground in which the modern psychological conceptions of human identity can take root and shape the scientific framework that constitutes the human reality. In the process, however, modern scientists have created an arbitrarily closed system that speculates upon the mysteries of mind, the origins of human consciousness, and the true nature of universal

---

16. The Muslim mystic Rumi ironically observed the contrary idea: "It is reason which has destroyed the reputation of the Intellect" (quoted in Seyyed Hossein Nasr, *Sufi Essays* [Albany, NY: SUNY Press, 1991], p. 55).

reality with all the naiveté and temerity of a child who is fully ensconced in the veracity of its own world without realizing the extent of the vast cosmos beyond the limited horizon of its mind.

The faculty of reason navigates its way through the investigation and discovery of the laws of nature; it sifts the sands of its inquiry, makes assumptions that advance its thinking, speculates upon the heart of the matter in question, quantifies its premises into mathematical formulations, generalizes its findings concerning the laws of nature into universal patterns, and ultimately articulates into a contemporary worldview the knowledge of higher principles scientists claim to have uncovered.

Yet, an alarming paradox strikes at the heart of the perception of what human powers of reason can accomplish: is human reason and thus a discerning intelligence something fundamental or is it subject to the contingency of evolution? Does it have the power to establish universal laws and principles and, if so, what standard does it abide by? Can it identify the truth and objectify reality? Do the laws that scientists uncover resonate throughout the universe and within time as being truly universal? Is there a standard inherent in human reason that has the right to qualify the parameters of a worldview such as the one set forth by modern science?

Needless to say, the modern-day conception of the nature and purpose of the faculty of reason has nothing to do with the phenomenon of the borderland of which we write. The modern conception of human reason sets boundaries that cannot be crossed, while the borderland of the spirit is a frontier wilderness in which the faculties of knowing and the fields of perception make the experience of the Ultimate Reality possible within the human frame of reference because it is a truth that exists to be experienced and "humanity as such" has the capacity to do so by virtue of these higher faculties. The modern concept of reason deals with the phenomenal and sensible world and attempts to process what those worlds deliver to its field of perception. As the mind's principal functional faculty, reason acts freely and autonomously within a closed system as if it had inherited certain inalienable rights, although the original source of that inheritance remains anyone's best guess. Not the least of these self-proclaimed rights is its professed ability to set the parameters of what we choose to believe and categorically deny as well as cast aside anything that does not fit that view.

In the modern era, reason has become the human faculty that is the final arbiter of the truth. As such, it is decisive in the formulation of all scientific knowledge. It serves as the criterion for what is true and what is false, for what is knowledge and what is ignorance, for what is intelligent and what is unintelligent. As the final arbiter of truth, the modern scientific worldview relies primarily on the faculty of reason in order to arrive at a true conception of the nature of things as they are in their true reality and not as they appear to be on the surface. This has led modern scientists down an unexpected pathway—to the very heart of the atomic elements which according to the new theories of quantum physics give way to a less than decisive theory of indeterminacy, whose very failure of predication is not the stuff of objectivity for which the scientific elite are looking in their verification of the universal principles of science.

Upon closer scrutiny, these claims to objectivity through the senses, to universality through the mind, and to the articulation of a "near absolute"[17] formulation through mathematics and natural law as the foundation to a relative world, produce a shallow echo of certitude that is "full of sound and fury, signifying nothing." Moreover, a paradoxical failure of logic emerges in which the mind itself not only attempts to place limits on the mind, but also then insists on such limits as the basis and the best of its logic.

In truth, there is an overwhelmingly subjective, contingent, and relative flavor to all that human reason proclaims and consequently to much of the worldview that modern science sets forth as a fully comprehensive system of knowledge and as a framework for action. It is true that reason pursues a line of logic, exhibits a profound capacity for mathematical formulation, and offers an exacting and progressive vision of the future with cutting-edge technology as the measure of its success. In addition, reason could be understood to have a subjective rather than an objective quality validating its findings, particularly the reason of modern times, without the irradiating factor bestowed upon the traditional concept of reason through the intellect and the intelligence. This is partly because everything the rational mind generates emerges from the contingent knowledge of this world alone, and partly because as an inflexible and closed system working on its own, the rational mind functions

17. Some scientists actually express a fear of arriving at an "unassailable definition of objective truth" because it "smells of absolutism" (E. O. Wilson, *Consilience*, p. 70)

within a climate that refuses to acknowledge a supra-rational source for all the principles—whether they be scientific, mathematical or otherwise—found within the natural order.

In order for a river to flow, it must have an origin and source. In order for the faculty of reason to function and exhibit some kind of meaningful directionality, it must also have a starting-point and primary source of knowledge that it can draw upon for its inspiration and light. Contrary to public expectation, however, the faculty of reason in its modern conception has no well-defined starting point and no credible source of knowledge other than the premises and propositions placed upon the *tabula rasa* of its field of vision by modern-day rationalism. Unlike the intuitive knowledge of the human intellect, which according to the various traditions represents a direct and immediate descent from above, discursive knowledge is basically synonymous with indirect and mediate knowledge, which is the mainstay of human reason, a knowledge that is gained by participation in the cognitive process alone. It cannot find within itself the guarantee of its own truth, but instead must receive this guarantee from principles that surpass it. Otherwise, it is merely the individual mind attempting to define supra-individual realities on its own together with a faculty of reason that wears a wizard's cap.

What is the first premise that generates the cognitive process? What underlies its preliminary theories and suppositions with a foundation of certitude? From where does it derive its authority, much less its certitude? What is the source of its knowledge, what Plato called the *arche anypothetos*,[18] his first principle or the Absolute? Is the question of the criterion of objective truth merely a physical problem amounting to an empirical question that can be answered by probing the physical basis of the thought process itself? Or is it a philosophical problem whose answer lies within the higher faculty of intellect to be able to recognize and respond to the original source and final word for what is objective, true, and absolute?

The modern-day faculty of reason, and the encompassing environment of rationality it inspires, cannot constitute the criterion of a truth or a falsehood because there is nothing intrinsic to any

18. Plato, *Republic* 510B-511B.

aspect of reason that could qualify it for such a role. Where can the guarantor of truth and the witness of its veracity be found? Who is the true observer within us who can rightfully assert that this is true and this is false, this is real and this is illusory. There must be within the mind a capacity of detached observer that has the power to transcend the individual order and the possibility of an impartial witness that can provide the objectivity of first principles and serve as the prefiguration for all certitude.

♣ ♣ ♣

Beyond the question of an arbitrary reductionism that searches through the remotest elements of the natural order in an effort to comprehend the totality of the cosmic reality; beyond the questions raised by quantum mechanics concerning the true nature of physical matter; and beyond the problem of a reality based solely on the concept of matter to the exclusion of all else, lies the meaning and significance of the human faculty of reason within this speculative context. When we say that humans themselves have become the criterion of reality, we refer of course to the faculty of reason within the mind, which provides the operative framework and rational basis for establishing this objective reality. From the traditional point of view, this assumption is considered a highly questionable point of departure, suggesting that there is no higher faculty within humanity other than the faculty of reason. The modern scientific worldview makes matters worse by suggesting that reason is both *tab ula rasa* and *end station* of the mind, the rarefied arena for the prefiguration of all knowledge and the final transfiguration of the mind into the witness and harbinger of truth.

As a kind of *tabula rasa* of the mind, reason is portrayed as a neutral faculty that has its own integrity but that does not suffer the intrinsic emotion, confusion, uncertainty, and doubt that are the inevitable characteristics of the human condition. As the operative receptacle of all thoughts and impressions, reason is understood to be free of the all too familiar condition of inner turmoil that is embodied in the human ego and summarized in the conflicting emotions of our daily lives. As such, we imagine in our fantasy that the faculty of reason is unencumbered by any outside influence and unobstructed by the psychological knots or complexes that may confront the emotional and psychic systems of the mind. This, of course, must be the very stuff of a modern-day mythology. As *end station* of the mind, it sweeps away any challenge to its authority by proclaiming that there is nothing real in an objective world other than what the human reason itself can establish and process through the senses. Needless to say, what distinguishes the two philosophies of the secular and traditional worlds is the distinction that exists between reason and the capacity of the intellect to enlighten the rational mind with the first principles that form the basis of all thought.

From the point of view of traditional wisdom, reason possesses only a dialectical and not an illuminative function; it is therefore not capable of grasping that which lies beyond the world of forms. The fault lies not with its traditional ability but with its modern-day interpretation and application. The modern scientific worldview claims that reason can deal with the origin and source of our existence and our fundamental reality without opening itself to the higher levels of perception made available by the direct intuitions of the human intellect. The intellect has traditionally been understood to be the faculty through which humanity apprehends and experiences the metaphysical and eternal realities. However, modern science is not interested in these metaphysical and eternal realities. With no use for these astounding truths, the scientific establishment simply pretends, indeed insists, that they do not exist. Scientists adhere to the party line that their discipline is a rational one, just as their form of knowing resides within the physical rather than the metaphysical plane.

However, the denial of the existence of the intellect leads to a conceptual chasm between the seen and unseen realities, and this is nearly impossible to bridge in the modern world:

> The external world of matter and the internal world of mind, if you will, have then seemingly lost their connection; and this means, of course, that the universe, and our position therein, have become *de facto* unintelligible. It is the nature of reason to analyze, to cut asunder even, it would seem, what God Himself has joined; no wonder, then, that a *Weltanschauung* based upon reason alone should turn out to be fractured beyond repair.[19]

19. Wolfgang Smith, *The Quantum Enigma* (Peru, Ill.: Sherwood Sugden & Company, 1995), p. 16.

It is as if the power of observation, the cognitive abilities of the mind, and the immediacy of sensory experience have constructed a kind of "wall of prejudicial truth" that arbitrarily excludes the faculty of the intellect with its concomitant perceptions of the higher realities. From the point of view of modern science, beyond this wall of truth nothing exists; indeed, nothing is considered real unless it is measurable and can be expressed via mathematical formulation. Observational experiments can be conducted and believed in without the alleged deceptions and vague promises of a blind religious faith.

Once again, more questions emerge that need addressing by the scientific community. Was modern science then born as a form of worship of our purely sensorial experience? What precisely does modern science ask of us? Does it ask us to believe in a homogeneity of knowledge that results in the certain reduction of the qualitative aspects of nature to quantitative modalities? If so, then modern science asks us to sacrifice a good part of what is, according to the various traditions, the reality of the universe. In compensation, it offers us a mathematical schema whose major advantage is to help us manipulate matter on the plane of quantity, without however taking into account or realizing the qualitative consequences that have had such disastrous results for humanity in the modern world.

Why does modern science ask so little of its devotees? Indeed, one could rightfully ask: why does it ask so much if it proposes to narrow the scope of a universal knowledge to the ability of reason to determine what is a valid experience through the human senses? Doesn't this attitude effectively eliminate all of the qualitative and spiritual richness of the universe, as well as the world of the spirit within us? Is the human being all mind and matter, dependent on the chemical fusions of the brain and the implicit intelligence of cellular DNA, leaving humans bereft of the benediction of the higher planes of spiritual intelligence, intuition, soul, and spirit?

After a careful study of the contemporary research concerning the nature of the mind and the implicit consciousness that makes us what we are, a person cannot help but come away with a feeling of profound ambivalence concerning the modern conception of humanity because this ambivalence lies at the heart of the modern worldview and is reflected within the social norms and ethical behavior of modern society. What people today seem to want is a rational and empirical explanation that can define what a human being is and to what purpose the species of *Homo sapiens* is supposed to function. Yet, for all of its advanced powers of observation, its incredible single-mindedness of approach, its miraculous discoveries, its technical powers, and its broad diversity of expression, modern science still has no clear idea about the true nature of humanity. What escapes its scrutiny are the very things that define a human being's identity, that characterize his individual human nature, and that ultimately qualify his unique humanity.

The overwhelming question in neurobiology today is the relation between the mind and the brain. Most neuroscientists now believe that all aspects of mind, including its most puzzling attribute—consciousness, and its complement awareness—are likely to be explainable in a more materialistic way as the behavior of large sets of interacting neurons. Still, it is precisely because there are mysterious aspects to the nature of the human mind, to consciousness, and to the presence of an awareness that seems to elude all physical description, that people living in today's world still remain basically unsatisfied with the scientific explanation of the mind and of human consciousness as purely a manifestation of the chemical activity of the physical brain. The irony lies in the fact that in its single-minded attempt to reduce all the miraculous interaction of the body, mind, and heart to the machinations of chemicals and neurons, science has inadvertently revealed a deeper world of mystery that is not yet ready to give up its secrets. The deeper our scientific understanding becomes of the inner world of the mind, the more profound the mystery that is revealed.

Before closing this chapter, it is worth noting in passing that physicists, who are perhaps most familiar with the mysterious ways in which matter actually behaves, tend to take a less mechanistic view of the world than do biologists and are actually taking the lead in articulating a new scientific paradigm that can lead the way beyond the old thinking of the classical and mechanical scientific worldview into a new age science that is less dogmatic and more attuned to the realities of nature it sets out to describe. Biologists have been steadily moving toward a hard-core kind of materialism as a result of the reductionist approach that attempts to reduce the human mind and spirit to a series of atoms and molecules. They have invested so much in the theory of evolution that for them to abandon it now would be perceived by the life science people as a form of intellectual suicide. The insistence on the spontaneous and indeed miraculous emergence of the life force within inanimate nature against all statistical probability and the discontinuous transmigration of species from a single-celled organism to sophisticated humans attests to the fact that modern scientists will go to any lengths to maintain the basis of their assumptions.

Physicists, on the other hand, have come to realize through their relentless analysis of the fundamental building blocks of matter that we do not even know anymore where a particle ends and where a wave begins, a phenomenon that lies at the heart of the quantum mystery. The true nature of matter has become indeterminate in such a way that the true nature of the mystery has finally been revealed. Some scientists are increasingly preparing themselves for the eventuality that our scientific criteria and methods of observation may have to undergo some subtle but important shift and begin to take account of certain clues that may present themselves in unexpected ways in areas of understanding that may initially seem to be beyond the scope of science *per se.*

Roger Penrose, a well-known British mathematician who has written extensively on the mystery of the mind,[20] falls back from embracing a new scientific paradigm of knowledge and relies on the following comment which really summarizes the heightened feeling of ambivalence that lies at the heart of this difficult issue. He writes:

> It may well be that in order to accommodate the mystery of mind, we shall need a broadening of what we presently mean by science, but I see no reason to make any clean break with those methods that have served us so extraordinarily well.[21]

Scientists may be reluctant to realize that a paradigm shift may happen not so much as an accommodation to the mystery of the mind as an accommodation to the mystery of the scientific attitude that all truth must be reduced to a rational and empirical standard of thought in order to adjure its validity.

20. *The Emperor's New Clothes* (1989) and *Shadows of the Mind: A Search for the Missing Science of Consciousness* (1994) are among his most respected works on the subject.
21. Roger Penrose, *Shadows of the Mind* (Oxford: Oxford University Press, 1994), p. 50.

Perhaps the shift in perception will find its sufficient cause in the realization that what we know to be true by virtue of an inner experience cannot be described in the words of a determined rationalist by a top-down set of algorithmic rules and principles. Curiously enough, much of what we know and act upon is the result of what we call common sense, an inner knowledge amounting to a wisdom that is based partially on sound experience and partially on an accepted and universal perception of things which is the collective pursuit of the ages. The main failure of artificial intelligence to date has been in the common sense activities that the humblest of us indulge in every day of our lives. No computer-controlled robot can yet begin to compete with a young child in performing some of the simplest of everyday activities such as recognizing that a colored crayon is needed to complete a particular drawing. Even an ant could far surpass today's computer controlled systems in performing its daily activities. The mind, the will, and the self-awareness that we take for granted are perennial mysteries that cannot be accounted for by modern science. Common sense tells us that they exist, serve a useful purpose, and ultimately determine and define who we are in ways we may never fully understand.

If we could perceive and experience our lives with the unimpeded clarity of our higher or spiritual consciousness, we would be able to see and understand that no visible thing—indeed nothing belonging to the world of natural phenomena—possesses existence or being in its own right. We would see and understand that, apart from its inner dimension and its spiritual identity, matter on its own possesses no reality whatsoever, whether physical, material, or substantial. That the purely physical reality could come into being and exist on its own is a strictly modern conception that is the product of the ego-consciousness of this era and is the defining characteristic of our time.

The manner in which the faculty of reason is exercised during modern times is merely a reflection of the shadow self and not a reflection of the higher intellect that can perceive the truth directly. What, then, can lead human beings beyond the horizon of the individual self? For an answer, we must turn now to the inner world of higher intelligence in our search for a faculty with the power to transcend the limitations of the human mind. The faculty of reason, with the aid of an intelligence that finds its luminous source in the

Supreme Intelligence, and with the aid of an intellect that enjoys direct access to the knowledge of God, can fulfill its role as bridge between worlds within the borderland of the spirit, dealing with the contingencies of this world and with the illumination of the world of the spirit. It can serve as one faculty among a number of other faculties that make the totality of the human experience possible in the first place.

If we take this modern-day reliance on reason back down into the well of our being in order to reach its source, we may be startled by what we discover. If there is a mystery at the center of our being, then we must use all the means at our disposal, including our mind, our intelligence, our reason, our heart, our imagination, our emotions and not least the sacred sentiments in order to come to terms with that mystery. The mystery that lies deep within the well of the human being is the mystery of existence itself, whose resolution can only be found in the experience of being oneself within the totality of one's true nature and being.

Ultimately, the spiritual traditions may have the final answer to the dilemma of reason as an instrument of enlightenment. They envision the faculty of reason as a two-sided face, one side illuminated by the rays of the intellect and the product of its divine reflection, the other side a dark hinterground of logic and causality whose self-reflection produces shadows that run the risk of actually creating an eclipse of the intellect rather than reflecting its light. In the traditional context, the faculty of reason serves as the bridge between the two worlds of logic and transcendence, giving rise to a conviction, like a lamp beckoning in the darkness of some vast prairie, that there is a knowledge whose certitude cannot be denied, whose source lies far beyond the horizon of the human mind, and whose realization within the human heart is destined to become the final emotion and the most enduring one.

Chapter Two

♣

The Luminous Source
of Human Intelligence

God is Intelligence occupied with knowing itself.
  (Meister Eckhart)

He who is learned is not wise; He who is wise is not learned.
  (Tao Te Ching)

Within the borderland of the spirit, beyond the first tier of human reasoning, lies a sun door that leads to the mysterious if not downright mystifying faculty of intelligence. This is the human faculty that imparts to the inquiring mind a spiritual intuition that radiates with the perennial message of the direct knowledge of God, a sublime imperative that fuels the fire of the mind with the inner glow of the infinite and the eternal. We know enough about ourselves to realize that our intelligence, and its complement the mind, is the prime mover of our thinking and conscious selves; but precisely what forms its contents, how it operates, where it draws its first principles from, and what enables and sustains the vital flow of its complex and subtle activity remains a mystery without resolution. This is particularly so in the modern world in which many people refuse to consider the sacred paradigm of a knowledge that relies on the light of the first principles emanating from a divine Source to define the true nature of human intelligence. The secrets of the mind are still not forthcoming and may never be—at least not to a modern mentality long steeped within the tradition of mathematical precision and the uncompromising exclusivity of the scientistic approach to understanding the world.

As we hope to show throughout the course of this work, the balanced functioning of the human mind, its native intelligence, and the consciousness that provides the driving force of the human self-awakening needs inspiration and support from a source higher than itself, for the mind on its own is a *tabula rasa* of human potential waiting to be awakened and become fully expressive. Left to its own devices, human intelligence is an uncertain faculty in search of a medium of true understanding, bereft of the wisdom of the ages and deprived of the spark and afterglow of an initial first knowledge.

According to the traditions of the perennial philosophy, the source of such knowledge originates within the vertical dimension, whose axis intersects the horizontal plane of this world like a flaming sword from heaven and whose insight has perennially provided people the means to confidently navigate the dark realms that exist in the labyrinth of the mind. This first knowledge, experienced within the mind as a mysterious and incisive light, descends from above as the luminous source of intelligence that casts revelatory rays of light across the surface of the mind like the whirling beams of a lighthouse, illuminating some stormy promontory of the mind. Every thought in the light of those celestial rays seems to have something infinite behind it; every object seems to abide in its appointed place.

Perhaps it is symptomatic of the era in which we live that modern humanity does not seem to realize that it cannot fit the totality of the human mind into a strictly rational and purely physical mold. Conscious experience is portrayed in today's world as a physical and not a supernatural phenomenon while the mind, which comprises both human consciousness in addition to rational processes, is actually considered by the prevailing materialistic outlook to be neural activity at work within the brain and nothing more. How can the possibility of a transcendent human intelligence be brought home to people for whom intelligence is nothing but a means of acting out the dictates of matter and whose search for knowledge culminates solely in the explanation of phenomena within the natural order? Are contemporary scientists, as the high priests of our rational and technological culture, willing to reduce our humanity solely to the activity of neurons and neurotransmitters as the basic building blocks in their construction of a grand synthesis of a theory of mind?

Innumerable signs to the contrary suggest that the mind is much vaster than we are now accustomed to envisage. Neither the approach of reductionism nor the evidential neural activity of the brain will ever be enough to satisfy the profound indications of a supra-rational faculty that substantiates the true functioning of human intelligence, the powers of mind, and the prescience of a heightened consciousness that actually set humanity on a course toward self-realization and transcendence. Darwin held the view that "animals have an intellect of different proportions" and that the "intellectual faculties have been mainly and gradually perfected through natural selection." He also wrote: "I see no difficulty in the most intellectual individuals of a species being continually selected, and the intellect of the new species thus improved. . . . I look at this process as now going on with the races of man; the less intellectual races being exterminated."[1] According to Darwinian evolution, chance and random mutations within the brain, eons of geological time, and the mysteriously anticipatory forces of natural selection have all conspired[2] to ultimately create what we now experience as the miracle of the mind and its multiple layers of conscious awareness—a happily fortuitous accident, to say the least.

For all its technical wizardry and in spite of the reams of detail intended to substantiate its validity and its ultimate veracity, the modern, scientific viewpoint is not particularly enlightened in its approach to articulating not only the origin of human intelligence, but also its very nature and purpose. In order to somehow come to terms with the mystery and miracle of the higher faculty of intelligence, the reductionist tendency of modern scientists articulates a sequence of explanations that quickly moves downward from the lofty regions of the mind to the brain to neural activity to anatomical structure, cellular physiology, molecular biology, and ultimately comes to rest on a firm bedrock in the laws of quantum mechanics, rather than upward through the arena of the human psyche to the realms of higher consciousness, to the soul and ultimately the spirit of man that in the Islamic perspective draws upon the Breath (*al-nafas*) of the Compassionate (*al-Rahman*).

1. Quoted in Rama Coomaraswamy, *In Quest of the Sacred*, eds. S. H. Nasr and Katherine O' Brien (Oakton, Va: Foundation for Traditional Studies, 1994), p. 103.
2. A conspiracy that ended, it should be pointed out, with the end of the evolutionary process itself. It may surprise a few people to learn that there is no definitive evidence substantiating the claim that an evolutionary process as a grand progression of trans-species development, envisaged by Darwin and perpetuated by modern-day biologists, has ever happened. Lynn Margulis, Distinguished University Professor of Biology at the University of Massachusetts, says that history will judge neo-Darwinism as "a minor twentieth-century religious sect within the sprawling religious persuasion of Anglo-Saxon biology." When she lectures to her fellow biologists, she often asks them "to name a single, unambiguous example of the formation of a new species by the accumulation of mutations. Her challenge goes unmet" (Quoted in Michael J. Behe's *Darwin's Black Box* [New York: Simon & Schuster, 1996], p. 26).

As a consequence, thinking has become a neurochemical process or, as the evolutionist E. O. Wilson says, "an epiphenomenon of the neuronal machinery of the brain."[3] As such, all the qualitative and profound richness of human intelligence as it was understood within the traditional world has been reduced to neuronal networks based solely within matter, which manifest as "points of energy" at source and nothing more, without reference to the creative spark, the incandescence of intuitive thought, the burning flame of cognitive reasoning, and the rich afterglow of higher consciousness of mind that forms the distinctive coloration of our humanness and qualifies us to be both the symbolic bridge between terrestrial and celestial worlds and the human representative of God on earth within the borderland of the spirit.

In coming to terms with the complexity of the mind, particularly in view of the newly perceived dependence of mind on matter, the latest by-word within the scientific community is the word "artificial." Science writers now refer to AI and AE as though these letters were old friends; indeed they may soon be. For those who are still unfamiliar with these terms, the acronyms refer to none other than artificial intelligence and artificial emotion. Even more troubling, when artificial intelligence and artificial emotions are mentioned: can an artificial human mind be far behind?[4] The 1996 chess contest between Deep Blue, an advanced chess-playing computer with a grand master status, and the then reigning world champion Gary Kasparov has been well documented and is well known. Using a 32 microprocessor to examine two hundred million chess positions each second is one thing; arriving at an artificial medium of thinking with the empowerment to simulate all the domains of human thought is quite another.

If the essence of human intelligence and its medium of the mind really can be reduced to organized matter that has, for want of a better term, the presence of mind to become points of energy with the power to initiate the human thought process, then an inter-

3. E. O. Wilson, *On Human Nature* (Cambridge, MA.: Harvard University Press, 1978) p. 195.
4. "Finally, given that conscious experience is a physical and not a supernatural phenomenon, might it be possible to create an artificial human mind? I believe the answer to this philosophically troubling question to be yes in principle, but no in practice, at least not as a prospect for many decades or even centuries to come" (E. O. Wilson, *Consilience*, p. 132).

esting question emerges. What would be the defining characteristics of such a modern intelligence and what would be the implications of such a medium of mind? Mental acumen and its companion, cognitive virtuosity, come immediately to mind as being the result of a mindless spontaneity of aroused neurons, together with an implicit—perhaps one should say diabolical—cleverness, a sharp incisiveness, and a love of meticulous exactitude, qualities much beloved by modern-day sophisticates. The highly valued play of mathematics captures the spirit of modern intelligence along with a fanatic and enduring willingness to process and absorb detail, particularly if it leads along the knife-edge of an innovative and practical technology that can add comfort as well as status to our lives. The modern mind loves the precision and the progressive quality of logic to order thought patterns along linear lines of perception, while modern intelligence would not be what it is without humanity's finely tuned ability, not only to quantify, but also to deal with abstractions that form elaborate architectures of speculative and theoretical thought. Finally, modern intelligence displays the capacity to process complicated thought patterns together with the ability to handle new and unstructured situations in a mechanical and automated manner that is in keeping with the mechanical and law-abiding features of matter.

Modern human beings have staked a tremendous claim onto the bedrock of their human intelligence, which itself is the result of a process of quantification—to quantify the very essence and mystery of all life processes. Indeed, given the extent to which today's scientists have developed the newly emerging technologies, including microchips driving everything from computers in the home to mega-telescopes that circle the globe surveying the wonders of outer space, the modern scientist has every right to be proud of what has been accomplished. Were it possible for a person from a previous century to be catapulted forward in time to the present era, they would undoubtedly suffer a form of culture shock as profound as the human mind could possibly endure. While they might remain intact, they would never remain the same; and neither has the modern psyche that is presently passing through a rate of technological change never before experienced on the globe. Yet, who can calculate the effect of these developments on the mind and the price that may have to be paid for these wondrous scientific and technological achievements?

The truth is that human beings have never been so technically adept, so mentally sharp, and so physically developed as they are today. Paradoxically, however, they have become morally questionable in their manner of behavior, unnatural in their manner of living, and spiritually alienated in their manner of thinking in today's post-modern world. This is reflected primarily in their attitude toward intelligence and what it means to be intelligent. The fundamental disbelief in a well-defined, multi-layered consciousness and a balanced sense of the true significance of the intelligence and what it can achieve would astound the unsuspecting ambassador from a previous era of time far more than the delightful wizardry of a television set or the miracles of modern communication such as mobile phones or the Internet. Is it intelligent to work within a closed system in the face of an overwhelming mystery? Is it intelligent to expect or want the emergence of life from an inanimate object? Is it intelligent to imagine that these supra-individual powers are determined by the forces of matter? Is it intelligent to reduce the primal force of the living being to the indeterminate forces within the world of quantum mechanics, running the risk of becoming an object for scientific scrutiny rather than the soul and spirit that the human entity is in principle?

Technical prowess and other innovative applications of the mind do not define what human intelligence is; nor do they satisfactorily explain the ultimate origin of the illuminating power of intelligence to recognize the truth that underlies all knowledge. To say human intelligence is already to identify its unique and most distinctive feature: the very faculty within the human being that distinguishes men and women from the rest of the organic kingdom by virtue of their ability to have recourse to the power of discernment bestowed upon them by God as an innate quality of human intelligence. Human intelligence is the prime mover in the discernment between what is real and what is illusory, between what is absolute and what is relative, between what is true and what is false, and between what is good and what is evil. As such, then, human intelligence not only defines humanity by virtue of what it is, knows, and does; it also shapes what human beings hold to be true in terms of value and meaning. It is the faculty of human intelligence that transforms an ordinary individual into a visionary person, a discerning person, a knowing person, and an ethical person rather than a primitive, savage, aboriginal, and/or wild animal that survives through a functional and instinctive intelligence.[5]

Human intelligence is a conduit of knowledge and perception that everyone wants in order to enjoy the many prospects that life has to offer, that everyone needs in order to navigate their way through the challenges and turmoil of life's progress, that everyone admires when it shines forth its illuminating insight, and that no one will admit to being without lest they fail to meet the distinguishing mark of their true humanity. Nevertheless, the faculty of intelligence has created a major controversy among individuals today as regards its true meaning and import. The well-known British scientist and mathematician, Roger Penrose, in a lengthy work exploring the true nature of the mind, confesses at one point that the ultimate origin and meaning of human intelligence escapes a definitive resolution. He writes with surprising frankness:

> Perhaps we should seriously consider the possibility that our intelligence might indeed require some kind of act of God—and that it cannot be explained in terms of that science which has become so successful in the description of the inanimate world.[6]

In other words, we still have no clue what it is precisely, how it functions, what its ultimate purpose is, and from where it draws its luminous coloration, including shades of brilliance that in fact have the power to illuminate the remotest, the darkest, and the most adamantine reaches of the human mind?

According to the perennial wisdom of the major world religions, human intelligence distinguishes itself from all other intelligences exhibited in the world of nature by virtue of its power of discernment, this being none other than the power to *know*—without any doubt and with a certainty—the Truth, the Reality, the Absolute, and the Good in both a substantive and an objective manner, since

---

5. Animal intelligence permits birds to build nests and travel great distances in seasonal flights of migration. Plant intelligence permits the face of the sunflower to "instinctively" follow the course of the sun as it traverses the heavens. Cellular intelligence organizes patterns of activity that ultimately create a wide variety of living organisms, much to the amazement of human intelligence; but none of these intelligences expresses the power of "discernment," namely the characteristic that gives intelligence its primary meaning within the human context.
6. Roger Penrose, Shadows of the Mind, p. 144.

it is the true, the real, the absolute, and the good that runs through the universe and through humanity itself like a cosmic Ariadnean thread,[7] connecting the created universe and everything in it with its origin and source in the Creator. In addition to this higher level of discernment that substantiates intelligence and that is concerned primarily with first principles, there lies within the intelligence the more pragmatic discernment that pertains to certain existential facts here on earth. The former refers to the intuition of metaphysical realities; the latter applies to the recognition of elements of the phenomenal world and their relation to higher orders of thinking and intuition. Thus, the human power of discernment permits a person to cultivate a sense of proportion on the plane of earthly phenomena, while the symbolist and abstract discernment of the truth keeps a person focused on "the one thing needful" (Luke 10:42).

Many other modes of intelligence exist that form a patchwork quilt of cognitive reasoning and creative adaptability within all phenomenal life forms in coming to terms with a variety of ontological and existential realities. Through the individual fields of modern science, we study and analyze the patterns and designs exhibited within nature for clues to the principles and laws of an ultimate intelligence that can account for the implicit intelligence we see evidenced everywhere in the creation. The laws of physics, chemistry, biology, and geology amount to little windows on the world that make sense of a portion of reality without identifying the source of cognitive discernment within humanity or revealing the true nature of the superior intelligence behind every created thing within the universe.

Paleontologists marvel at the tool-bearing ability of the primitive anthropoid apes, while zoologists wonder at the deftness and sagacity of modern-day gorillas that are able to use sticks as tools of retrieval to catch unsuspecting ants deep in their underground nests, suggesting a human-like intelligence that acts as a forerunner and link to the real intelligence of *Homo sapiens*. Does the gorilla's intelligence, however, overshadow in some way the intelligence exhibited in the dance of the bumblebee or the incredible flight

7. Theseus, the champion of Athens, walked into the Cretan labyrinth and was able to negotiate the twists and turns by unraveling a ball of thread given him by Ariadne, the lovestruck daughter of King Minos. By following the thread, he was able to retrace his steps out of the labyrinth after killing the Minotaur.

paths of migratory birds who travel great distances and require a rarefied form of intelligence, in addition to sheer endurance, to accomplish their journeys and bring them to their destination? Aren't these merely examples of other modes of intelligence whose miraculous ability traces its origin back to the supreme mind of God rather than to an evolutionary line of higher development? The fact is that animal intelligence displays an instinctive knowledge which is native to a given species; an intelligence that is non-reflective to be sure, but that derives its substance not from automatic reflexes within the body, but from the formal and qualitative aspect of the species itself, from its God-given qualities of being. The intelligence witnessed in animals that permits them to function within their own particular domain does not have to mean that they are our ancestors and we their descendents because they display intelligence suggestive of being a signpost or progressive link in the development of cerebral and cognitive abilities.

In fact, at every level in the hierarchy of being, we can witness forms of intelligence within nature that reflect the natural instincts that are required for natural phenomena to exist and function within their own sphere of experience. The message of a hidden wisdom shines forth in the corporeal intelligence that manifest throughout the human body in a multitude of cellular, chemical, and neural activity.[8] The intelligence of the macrocosm shines forth in the vast array of heavenly bodies and the spectacular and harmonious precision that is witnessed in the celestial movement of the cosmos. Sensory intelligence identifies and appreciates gourmet tastes; olfactory intelligence recognizes a wide array of smells and responds to them on a number of levels, including memory and emotion; even the intelligence of the sense of touch knows the difference between the natural fibers of cotton and the artificial feel of polyester, as everyone who lives in a tropical climate fully appreciates.

8. "Molecular biology has shown that even the simplest of all living systems on earth today, bacterial cells, are exceedingly complex objects. Although the tiniest bacterial cells are incredibly small, weighing less than 10^{-12}gms, each is in effect a veritable micro-miniaturized factory containing thousands of exquisitely designed pieces of intricate molecular machinery, made up altogether of one hundred thousand million atoms, far more complicated than any machine build by man and absolutely without parallel in the non-living world" (Michael Denton, *Evolution: A Theory in Crisis* [Bethesda, Md.: Adler & Adler, 1985], p. 250).

Every living thing expresses a form of intelligence that guides its functioning within a given domain; but only the human being knows with a prescience of mind that includes primary instinct, subtle logic, discursive reasoning, common sense,[9] insight, aesthetic appreciation, moral value, and ultimately the defining discernment that is uniquely human to the extent that it virtually defines humanity in terms of it's capacity to know. If true knowledge is there, then wisdom cannot be far behind; if morality is there, then virtue will show its sublime face; and if discernment is there, then true intelligence will shine forth as a fully formed creative power that embodies all the elements already evidenced in nature and that are reflective of a higher intelligence—the "supremely Intelligible," in the words of Frithjof Schuon.

Human intelligence is cast under the spell of a reflective consciousness that forms the backcloth of self-awareness and is charged by the heightened setting in which this intelligence functions. As such it is the fundamental and defining element of the humanity within the human being and is not a vestige or contingency of some random evolutionary process. Human intelligence—the primary manifestation of inward activity and thus the direct reflection of the inner being—becomes therefore the focal point and catalyst of how people identify themselves. Are we to understand human intelligence as a purely cognitive activity, displaying a mercurial tendency to wander in search of an equilibrium that is perfectly capable of being carried away by waves of endless speculation or extinguished in the devouring flames of an unfulfilled and possibly irrational emotion?

We marvel at the precision of the human mind of today, with its capacity for the exactitude of mathematics and its penchant for enduring the detail of innumerable dry facts; but we are equally concerned about its capacity for restless and unrequited movement, without ever being satisfied by the play of its formulations as it

9. Extensive research has gone into the development of artificial intelligence in the last twenty years, but the most unexpected and telling criticism to date is that it has not been successful in modeling what is known as common sense. David Waltz has pointed out in an article in *Scientific American* that no machine has yet been constructed that can mimic the cognitive capacities of the human brain: "Substantially better models of human cognition must be developed before systems can be designed that will carry out even simplified versions of common-sense tasks. I expect the development of such models to keep me and many others fascinated for a long time" (Quoted in Michael Denton, *Evolution: A Theory in Crisis*, p. 339).

passes from concept to concept in a desperate search for the virtue of consistency and the grace of certitude to be found within the traditional conception of mind and its implicit intelligence.

♣ ♣ ♣

The question of genuine sources for the first principles of knowledge strikes at the heart of the very definition and meaning of human intelligence. What indeed is the source of human intelligence? From where does human intelligence derive its vast array of characteristics, including its clarity and its brilliance, its knowledge and insight, its power of abstraction and reflection, its adaptability, its creativity and its vision, in short: its ability to process a vast range of conceptions, abstractions, and emotions through the medium of a self-reflective and abstract language in order to articulate in words this unique assemblage of qualities?

It is not for nothing that the litany of the mind's attributes has commenced with clarity and brilliance since the traditional view has long espoused the belief that human intelligence has an illuminative aspect that derives from a luminous source within the Universal Spirit. This is in sharp contrast to today's view which claims that human intelligence takes root in the faculty of reason, which provides individuals with the ability to think through any problem based upon an empirical method of inquiry, without independent principles of thought that transcend the limits of the operative mind. In truth, human intelligence has two sources of knowledge: it relies on both the intellect and reason, *ratio* and *intellectus*, to reflect upon the order of the natural world and alternatively to transcend it. The sibylline clarity of human intelligence represents an expression of mind that derives its substance and objectivity from the font of certainty that is characteristic of the truth, while its brilliance is the lunar reflection of the symbolic sun that is the Light of the universe.[10]

A knowledge that is objective and therefore fully independent of the multitude of subjectivities of this world and light years beyond the egocentricity of the human psyche needs a form of intelligence that draws its luminosity and its objectivity from an

10. In Islam, Light (*al-Nur*) is one of the ninety-nine names that identify the qualities and attributes of the Divinity. According to a well-known Quranic verse (24: 35), "God is the Light of the heavens and the earth."

impartial and principial source and has the capacity to process its content, not in a whimsical and relative manner based on the contingencies of human reason alone, but in an enlightened and absolute manner that draws on the first principles and has been sent forth and made available through the Supreme Intelligence of an Absolute Being.

> Intelligence has only one nature, that of being luminous. But it has diverse functions and different modes of working and these appear as so many particular intelligences. Intelligence with a "logical," "mathematical" or—one might say— "abstract" quality is not enough for attaining all aspects of the real.[11]

Far from being a one-sided and narrow faculty of perception amounting to a closed system of the mind that is exhibited within the modern worldview, human intelligence within the traditional perspective draws on a number of modalities that ultimately lead back to the origin and source of its illuminated insight.

In addition to bringing rational, reasonable, and common-sense factors to bear on its functioning, the *aql* of the Islamic traditions calls upon certain modalities of thought to complete the full complement of its intellective mold. Reason displays a reflective quality that brings to its line of thought all of the supportive documentation of the human emotions, the imagination, natural instinct, and a fundamental capacity for intuition that all take part in enriching the process of humanity's reasoning and in extending the human mind beyond its cognitive ability to encompass the possibilities of higher imagination, insight, inspiration, and creativity that is the very frontier of the borderland of the spirit. The full range of this intellective process can be achieved by none other than the use of the human *ratio* as a principle of coherence and the *intellectus* as a principle of transcendence as well as the source medium for direct access to the truth.

♣ ♣ ♣

Another question that needs to be asked in connection with these reflections on human intelligence and other rarefied functions

11. Frithjof Schuon, *The Essential Writings of Frithjof Schuon*, ed. Seyyed Hossein Nasr (New York: Amity House, 1986), pp. 113-114.

of the mind concerns the mind as matter and the mind as witness. What is the connection between the ancient and nebulous unicellular organism from which modern scientists wish to derive the entire animate world, and that self-reflective mirror that exists within the mind of humanity? "If human intelligence is not merely 'organized matter'—in which case it would not be intelligence— this means it necessarily participates in a transcendent principle."[12] Indeed, what has happened to the transcendent axis that once underscored the reality and the truth of all existence? Where is the impartial, objective backdrop behind the subjectivity of the human spirit and where is the witness and the guarantor of the truth in which we believe? Where can we discover the origin and source of the immutable criteria upon which we rely, even within our scientific systems? What is it within ourselves that has the unchallenged right to say this is true and this is false? If the answer is human reason, then it begs the question of the origin and source of such insight.

According to the traditional view, human intelligence exhibits a synthesizing quality that enables human beings to assimilate the knowledge of all the faculties with which it is associated in order to objectify themselves to the extent that they can see their own reflection and place it within an intelligible context. They can identify themselves with something other than themselves, and that they can know with an objectivity and a certitude that what they conceptualize is truthful and real. The coherent interaction of the faculties that come together and are summarized by the integrated functioning of an intelligent mind produces what scientists now refer to as consilience,[13] which is an explanatory power that derives part of its authority from a variety of disciplines. When the traditions accord human beings a central position within the cosmic frame of the hierarchy of being because of their human intelligence, this is what the traditions intend to convey: Through the functioning of their

12. Titus Burckhardt, "Cosmology and Modern Science," in *The Sword of Gnosis*, ed. Jacob Needleman (Baltimore: Penguin, 1974), p. 130.
13. Even E. O. Wilson, in setting the stage for the exposition of his major work entitled *Consilience*, resorts to religious terminology when speaking of his theme, in spite of his adamant attitude toward the religious spirit. "The belief in the possibility of consilience beyond science and across the great branches of learning is not yet science. It is a metaphysical worldview, and a minority one at that, shared by only a few scientists and philosophers" (p. 9).

mind, through the capacity of their intelligence, and through the practical power of their reason, subjective human beings can objectivize themselves with the criteria of a principial knowledge that is in the power of their intelligence to encompass, and thus exceed the specific and individual criteria that inevitably emerge within the human mind on its own.

In Islam, however, the faculty of reason (*aql*),[14] while displaying qualities that go far beyond the purely rational conception of human reason as the secular norm within a purely physical reality, is considered an intermediate and mediating faculty and not the final arbiter of truth that it is considered to be *de facto* in the contemporary Western worldview. There must be another, a higher faculty, that can transcend the inherent limitations of the faculty of reason; a faculty that has the power to witness the truth directly and the capacity to objectify—with a final certitude—things as they are in their reality. Aristotle has written: "Since scientific knowledge is by definition knowledge of causes, and since these first principles have no first causes, the ultimate foundation of scientific knowledge must be something other than scientific knowledge."[15] This higher faculty of the mind must have the power to place in perspective the totality of the truth. Its direct insight, and the conscious experience it has of the true nature of reality, can then seep down through the mind, the intelligence, and the reason to become an operative certitude guiding the life of humanity. Plato called this organ, with its capacity to witness a transcendent truth and intuitively grasp the first principles that underlie all of existence from the platform of certainty, the *nous*; Islam calls it the *aql*.

The line of direct perception commences with the Universal Intellect, alternatively called the Universal Spirit. According to the Prophet of Islam, the first thing that God created was the Intellect; thereafter, the Universal Intellect began to shine forth as if through a prism into multiple "lights" and manifested upon the earth in the form of revelation or the Word of God (*Kalimat Allah*), providing

14. The Quranic term *aql* keeps human beings on the straight path and prevents them from going astray. In the Quran, those who go astray are those who don't use the full extent of their reason (*wa la ya'qilun*) and thus are not able to understand what comes down to them from above.
15. *The Cambridge Companion to Aristotle*, ed. Jonathan Barnes (Cambridge: Cambridge University Press, 1995), p. 49.

human beings with the objective criteria needed to establish their place within the Divine Design. This knowledge then passed directly into the human intellect in such a way that the content of the inspiration is direct and immediate and has descended from the highest possible source imaginable, namely the Universal Spirit (Intellect), thus making human beings capable of objectivity, not by their own resources but through the empowerment of the Universal Intellect of the Divinity in an act of consilience of the highest order of magnitude.

The revelation, which is an objective knowledge that descends from the Mind of God, allows human beings, who are primarily subjective beings, to become truly objective. There is a direct encounter of the Divine Intellect with the human intellect, pouring into the receptive mold of the human intellect the essential contents of a knowledge that the intelligence needs in order to function according to its own true nature within the created world, touching the human mind with a magic wand that glows with the Divine Light, the *Prima Veritas*. As a result of that encounter, the conscious human mind is forever cast within the aura of this supreme knowledge whose essence substantiates all.

Within the collective schema of the descent of knowledge, the Universal Intellect is the metacosmic manifestation of the Supreme Unity. Revelation, as the exteriorization of the Divine Mind, is the macrocosmic manifestation of the Universal Intellect. As its complement on the earthly plane, the human intellect becomes the instrument of direct perception of the essential knowledge of God, including the first principle of His Unicity and the truth of the one Reality. As such, the human intellect is not something cerebral in the manner that we understand the human mind to be; nor is it a specifically human faculty in the sense that we understand the reason to be. Instead, it represents the spiritual faculty *par excellence* with a modality of perception that rises above the human dimension of this world in a kind of spontaneous act of transcendence that arrives at a vision of the Sublime Reality. The intellect does not rely on the reflective thinking process or the cognitive principles of reason; rather it is a receptive and synthesizing faculty, capable of knowing directly and intuitively without any cognitive undertaking and therefore capable of transcending individuals and their manner of thinking. Its revelatory power resolves the mystery underlying the source of true knowledge and its explanatory power conveys a feeling of overwhelming certitude that further verifies its objectivity.

If intelligence is the faculty of discernment, and if human reason is characterized as discursive and rational, then the intellect[16] is the faculty of direct perception and of contemplation. As the transcending faculty and the instrument of synthesis, the intellect is the highest faculty of perception that is available to humanity. Human reason is a faculty of the purely individual order; pure intellect is supra-individual. Without the transcending feature of the intellect, the capacity to conceptualize metaphysical knowledge would be impossible since such rarefied knowledge lies far beyond the range of the individual domain and is of the universal order. That metaphysical knowledge is accessible to the human mind lies in the fact that while we partake of the human order, we are also the manifestation of something far more miraculous. The being that we know ourselves to be in this world is also the expression of a different quality of person by virtue of the permanent and immutable principle that consecrates our deepest essence.

The intellect opens the gate of spiritual intelligence and its rarefied knowledge allows a person entry into the world of the spirit. Through the knowledge conveyed by revelation and received by the human intellect, every living person can know, with a certainty, their first origin and their final end. The dilemma surrounding the starting-point for all cognitive processes is resolved in a higher faculty that serves as the ultimate medium between converse worlds. The point of departure for all knowledge is established in the connection of the human intellect with the knowledge of the highest Principle and is confirmed in the Pure Intellect of the Divinity. The inner life of the individual, including all the natural instincts, spiritual imagination, sacred emotions, and higher consciousness— indeed the very faith human beings express in the Divinity—are fully awakened and receive the direct impress of the knowledge of

16. On the faculty of the intellect, Thomas Aquinas has written: "It must be said that just as to proceed *rationally* is attributed to *natural philosophy*, because in it there is observed most greatly the mode of reason, so to proceed *intellectually* is attributed to *divine science*, because in it there is observed most of all the mode of the intellect" [*Dicendum quod sicut rationabiliter procedere attribuitur naturali philosophiae, quia in ipse observatur maxime modus rationis, ita intellectualiter procedere attribuitur divinae scientiae, eo quod in ipse observatur maxime modus intellectus*] (*In Boetium de Trinitate*, q. 6, art. 1, ad. 3)

the Divine, thereby ushering into the higher consciousness of the mind and heart a knowledge of a complete and undivided Unity.

That human beings are much more than their bodies, more than the unique instrument of their mind, more even than the self-reflective wonder of their expansive consciousness, and that their knowledge extends far beyond the inquisitive ideas and analytical concepts deduced from the physical senses and orchestrated into a symphony of theoretical speculations, is taken as axiomatic by all the major world religions and their traditions. The power of the intellect permits people to transubstantiate their inner reality from an uncertain platform of tentative theory and speculation into an objectifying reality in order to raise themselves above the level of mundane awareness to a higher plane of consciousness and a more profound level of spiritual experience. It connects people directly with the supra-natural realities of a higher dimension, a power that passes from the human intellect to the created Intellect of Revelation and back once again into the vortex of the Universal Intellect where it lies steady and fully centered within the Godhead. It is truly the premier faculty of the borderland, connecting our immediate earthly world with the world of the spirit. It is the faculty that objectifies a person's subjective reality, the faculty that fully synthesizes the great disparity of this world with the Supreme Principle of the one reality of which this world is but a pale reflection and the stuff of which shadows are made.

The spiritual faculty of intuition, as the operative agent within the human intellect of a knowledge that is inaccessible to normal intelligence and thus the scientific methods of investigation, sheds its light on the mind and happens directly and unconsciously, without any seemingly formal apparatus, as a matter of spiritual instinct.[17] It enables people to perform the kind of mental tasks that they love to experience, but that they cannot account for consciously. We communicate through spoken and written words; we reason and think; we use our imagination and we dream. We plan and build cities; we farm land and feed ourselves and the world; we create literature and compose symphonies. We intuit imaginal

---

17. "The infallible 'instinct' of animals is a lesser 'intellect,' and man's intellect may be called a higher instinct" (Frithjof Schuon, *The Essential Writings of Frithjof Schuon*, ed. S. H. Nasr, p. 115).

worlds that have the power of reality and the certainty of knowledge. Mental processes are even coming to be recognized by some of the more enlightened thinkers of today as more intuitive than cognitive. Scientists themselves rely on the creative process of the mind and the imagination to initiate much of their probing, scientific inquiries. They would be loathe to admit it, but those sudden, intuitive illuminations could actually be lightning flashes of the soul that permit a person to move beyond the limits of their own shortcomings as a special dispensation from the Divinity.

Psychologists who research and study learning and behavior patterns are beginning to realize that people who feel and intuit their way through a challenging endeavor actually have a competitive edge over those who simply think their way through a problem in some straightforward rational manner. It often happens that those who intuit in this manner cannot specifically account for how they arrived at their conclusion. Mathematicians do not believe that they are blindly following unconscious rules that they are incapable of knowing and believing in; nor do they think that their reasoning is based on some arbitrary algorithmic procedure that—unknown to them—governs all of their mathematical perceptions. "What they think they are doing is basing their arguments upon what are unassailable truths—ultimately, essentially 'obvious' ones—building their chains of reasoning entirely from such truths."[18] They use their rational intelligence to make their way through complicated mathematical equations, but their intuitive intelligence could well be recognized as the dark light through which the unconscious first principles of mathematics arrive within the human mind.

Unsurprisingly, there is a vast difference between the knowledge arrived at through the efforts of human reason and the direct knowledge arrived at through the inimitable intuitions of the intellect. In today's post-modern age, human reason investigates the knowledge of this world. The intellect of those living in more traditional times participated in the knowledge of the world of the spirit. Both forms of knowledge pass through the human mind and are filtered through human intelligence as key components to the practical functioning of people in dealing with this world. Intuitive intelligence needs the practicality of the reason to cope with the

18. Roger Penrose, *Shadows of the Mind*, p. 127.

existentialities of this world, whereas the faculty of human reason needs the light of the intellect to make the essential knowledge shine forth as a guiding star in the dark firmament of the mind.

When our intelligence is cut off from its luminous source, our knowledge, our judgment, our insight, and indeed our sense of discernment will be seriously diminished during the course of life. Under these conditions, there is no way that these faculties can function to their fullest capacity, in accordance with what is true to human nature. Sadly, the modern mentality does not accord the intellect its true value as a spiritual faculty capable of direct knowledge of God. Although modern individuals still have an intellect, they do not know they have it; they therefore have nothing to effectively counterbalance the tenebrous inclination of the human mind to roam aimlessly through the dark and labyrinthine corridors of idle theory and pure speculation.

People today have the gift of intelligence and they enjoy its multitudinous fruits; of this there is no doubt. In today's modern world, however, we falter and hesitate in our definition of terms: What is the mind, what defines consciousness, what is the stuff of intelligence, and where will our intelligence lead us? We have the duty to ask ourselves not only whether consciousness, mind, and intelligence are enough to serve our needs, but also to what end? Opinions differ on the key fundamentals that shape the contemporary worldview and yet the goal seems to be the attainment of a knowledge that does justice to human intelligence: to be intelligent, to live intelligently, and to connect with the Supreme Intelligence with the golden thread of faith and desire. We need to free ourselves from an undue reliance on all speculative and ego-serving ideas whose only source is the human mind blundering on its own without the aid of heaven; we need to turn away from the downward drift of human pride and pretension and submit ourselves to that which surpasses us; we need to surrender to the divine paradigm of knowledge and the source of all wisdom that alone has the power to illuminate the mind and enlighten the heart.

A final thought leads us to reaffirm that behind the natural workings of the human intelligence lies a supra-natural source whose luminosity shines down on the mind—with all of its faculties of knowing and perception—like rays of light penetrating woodland trees to reach the forest floor. If reason is in principle a *tabula rasa* whose innocent void awaits a knowledge whose truth will awaken a world, then human intelligence is a playing field awaiting the illuminative rays of the intellect, the regal faculty within the kingdom of the mind, around which are gathered the ministers of state in the form of noble faculties including reason, intelligence, imagination, and the higher emotions. They all contribute to the qualitative expression of the human species; they all make human beings what they truly are. It is only because intelligence is touched by the light of the intellect that people can reflect upon their human condition and say: I am a thinking creature created as a reflected image of the Supreme Intelligence; I am a shadow of the Divine Light; I am a soul whose ground reflects the luminous rays of the Divine Spirit; I am a subjective entity capable of objectivity because the Absolute has taken up residence within the cave of my heart as the living principle of my being.

Meister Eckhart refers to that "light" which shines out from the essence, a light that can penetrate the "simple core" and the "still desert" within oneself, a light that reaches into the secret that no one has the right to know solely through their own designs. "This core is a simple stillness, which is unmoved itself but by whose immobility all things are moved, that is to say, all people who live by reason and have their center within themselves. That we, too, may live so intelligently, may God help us. Amen."[19]

19. *Meister Eckhart,* trans. Raymond B. Blakney (New York: Harper Torchbooks, 1941), p. 247.

Chapter Three

♣

The Other Heart, the Forgotten One

God cometh between a man and his own heart.
  (Quran 8:24)

The heavens and the earth cannot contain Me, but the heart of My
believing servant does contain Me.
  (Hadith qudsi)[1]

The human heart has always held a prominent place in coming to
terms with the true meaning implicit in the image of *Homo sapiens.*
Because of its symbolic value and its role as a higher faculty, the heart
has access to higher perceptions and spiritual insights that would otherwise remain inaccessible to the human mind on its own. Nothing
captures more effectively the essential character and the intrinsic
humanity of the human spirit than does the traditional symbol of the
heart. As seat of the intelligence and an instrument of enlightenment, it contains latent dispositions and powers that far exceed the
life-giving properties of the physical heart that lies within the breast.
    Within each of us lies a beating heart whose defining features
help to identify the true nature of a person through its numerous
modes of expression and its central role as a higher faculty of perception. Within each of us lies an embedded heart. Its presence
within the inner sanctum of the breast assures us that there is no
secret that the heart withholds from our understanding or experience. We remember and recognize within the depths of our hearts
all of the polarities that constitute the split personality of the human
being. We are hard-hearted and soft-hearted; we are tender-hearted
and cold-hearted; we are light-hearted and broken-hearted. We can
be all heart and heartless. When we wish to draw from deep within
our innermost depths, we reach down to the bottom of our hearts.
The heart is timid or brave, open or closed, cruel, kind, black or

1. A *hadith qudsi* is a Holy Tradition in Islam in which God speaks directly through
the Prophet. Like the Quran, *hadith qudsi* are understood to be the "word" of God.

pure. Each of these heart affinities are tendencies that every person understands, for they are modes of expression that actually identify qualities that lie at the core of the human being and that portray the essence of a person's moving self image.

Within the traditional perspective, the heart lies within a borderland between two visions of a single reality. One of these visions gazes outward upon the world in order to witness there an indirect image of reality through the symbols and signs of nature, which amount to a premonition of what lies behind that image. The other vision gazes inward toward the sacred center of the human being's personal, inner world in order to experience directly within the heart the universal vision of the one true reality. As such, the heart has a dual role and therefore a dual meaning. As the center of the individual in view of the outer world, it expresses the broad range of the human emotions based on the faith it expresses and the knowledge in which it chooses to believe. As the center of the individual in view of the inward dimension, however, it expresses its true centrality as the human microcosm of the transcendent Principle. It becomes the eye that sees and the seat of an intelligence that discerns and bears witness to the truth of the one Reality.

Nothing in nature reveals the symbolic transparency of matter more and nothing in human nature permits people to better perceive the inward reality of things, from the inverted angle of spiritual insight as it were, as does the human heart. If the instrument of the mind relies on the penultimate faculty of the intelligence and its principal well-spring, intuition, then the heart, as the seat of the intelligence and the niche of sacred sentiment, is the quintessential organ of human perception. It is a transcendent faculty that has the capacity to combine the essential knowledge of God with the heartfelt experience of the human being in order to internalize the fundamental unity that underlies all of universal reality.

The heart has traditionally been portrayed as a holy sanctuary of reflected light and a hidden cave in which there is sequestered all essential knowledge, all sacred emotion, and all intimate love in a manner that permits human beings to transcend their fragmented earthly likeness for a complete truth that summarizes the meaning of their being. As such, the heart's rarefied vision of the world has an inverse application that through the filter of an intuitive knowledge literally changes the phenomenal world from the brute physical matter that it appears to be into a living reality that it is by virtue of its connection to the knowledge of the Universal Reality.

Unlike modern humanity, which attempts to take leave of its being through the labyrinthine passageways of the mind, people in more traditional cultures believed that the point of departure from the confines of the individual self lay within the affective heart rather than the cognitive mind, much less the cerebral brain, which for modern humanity is the starting point and ultimately the highest organ that justifies the implicit *sapiens* within *Homo sapiens*. More traditional societies understood their existence to be the result of the existential manifestation of a Supreme Reality in which they took part on an individual level of experience. This existence was envisaged as having its point of first origin and its ultimate source in a Transcendent Being who was the central point beyond which all existence radiated outwards. This Supreme Being substantiated the mystery of His Spirit through the creation of the universe and came to be known through a humanity that populated and animated that universe as a conscious and thinking being capable of communicating with its Creator.

Humanity became invested with the vocation of being the earthly simulacrum of the celestial Being, who in return became the divine spark that dwells within the human heart and the holy breath that infiltrates every cell in the body, since the Quran confirms that God "breathed into him [Adam] of His Spirit" (15:29). The Divine Being as the Center of the macrocosm took up residence within the spiritual center of the individual being, the human microcosm of the heart-center. This powerful, symbolic image of centrality has taken shape and solidified as the organ of the heart that in representing humanity's individual centrality remembers the universal Center at the heart of all existence.

Within the traditional worldview, the search for the source of existence and for a source of knowledge of that Truth begins with the mind. The inquiry, the quest, and the vision of the intelligent person was firstly directed inwards, toward the center of the individual's own particular world, namely the world of the inward being as essentially summarized by three fundamental keys: the thoughts, emotions, and desires. These reflect the three key faculties of the human being: discerning intelligence, holy sentiment, and free will. This outlook on the world and the value of this worldly experience were tempered by the intensity of inner aspiration and the knowledge on which that aspiration was based. Since more traditional peoples were avowedly seeking the Kingdom of God, they went directly to the place where it could initially be found, namely "within you," in keeping with the well-known saying of Christ in the Gospels.[2]

Within the progressive, scientific worldview of today, the search for the source of existence and of the knowledge that empowers that existence with its principles and pragmatism, begins with matter and the universally accepted first principles of mathematics. The intelligent person of today turns exclusively outward toward the phenomenal world, not in its capacity to symbolize and contain an inner meaning or reflect a higher reality, but rather for the purposes of breaking down and analyzing its constituent elements in search of the knowledge of an objective reality and a universal theory that could explain the existence of that reality. How elements of a lower order can generate and qualify phenomena of the higher order is not a question that seems to concern the scientific establishment. The primary concern of the scientific endeavor lies in proving those things that exist with a pre-established set of criteria rather than existence as such and its possible meaning for humanity in view of its higher reality transcending the human order.

Within the contemporary scientistic mindset, observable facts serve as the criteria of an objective knowledge and human reason serves as the discriminating power that sets the inquiry in motion and organizes its findings into a plausible pattern of believability. What lies outside the ability of the human mind to formulate and prove scientifically lies outside the realm of objectivity. The mysteries of the universe—which traditional societies once held in awe and which fueled their imagination to transcend their natural limitations—now await public scrutiny and final resolution. Accordingly, reason will show the way, and progress through time will eventually solve the problem of the true nature of reality. To this end, scientists hope to discover some kind of fundamental law that governs the interaction of all phenomena and thereby arrive at the widely-sought unified theory of everything that would explain the true nature of the universe once and for all.

2. "*Regnum Dei intra vos est*" (Luke 17: 21). This recalls a similar conception in one of the Taoist texts (*Chuang Tzu*, ch. 22): "Do not ask if the Principle is in this or that. It is in all beings. Because of that, It is given the epithet of great, supreme, entire, universal, total."

The vision outward toward the external world is separative, fragmentary, and speculative, searching for a passageway deep down into the inner constituents of matter in the hope of arriving at the *materia prima,* the first cause and the universal substance, indeed the very heart of matter.[3] This modern-day approach relies precariously (and ironically) on a faith in the assumption that the mind can negotiate its way through the labyrinthine mysteries of the universe and arrive at the universal basis of matter *on its own terms.*

The vision inward toward the inner world of the spirit is discriminating, unitive, and total, searching for a passageway that will lead deep down into the central core of the human being to reveal a knowledge of the human condition and the universe that is unique, unitive, and universal. If humanity was a spool of thread that had been wound into the shape of a man or woman, then the end of that thread would lie buried deep within the center of their being as inviolate and sacrosanct. The end of that thread would constitute the origin, source, and center of the vital being, the point of departure of the lifeline and the very heart of the human entity. In the inverted angle of this perspective, unity becomes the sole reality, while the separativity and relativity of the world becomes the enduring illusion. That which truly endures can only be found at the end of the cosmic thread, at the primordial point and absolute center of Reality.

Every message of the heart, from its outer physiological and cardiac properties to its inward and interiorizing modalities of perception and sentience, proclaims the mystery of centrality in the light of the certitude of existence. It is a mystery of time and place that finds its inception and ultimate resolution within the heart of humanity, of nature, and of the universe generally. The heart plays this role of centrality in a multitude of venues, from its role as the utter core and essence of the phenomenal world such as when we speak of the heart of the atom or the heart of the earth, to its function as the central pump of the physical body circulating the lifeblood through the arteries and veins of the human corporeal system, to its articulation as the macrocosmic heart of the universe

3. Physicists have now delved so deeply into the world of quantum physics that they have laid bare the inner core of the atom only to discover the indeterminate theory of matter, revealing an unstable core rather than the primordial center they had hoped to unveil.

around which flows the magisterial procession of the celestial galaxies. The heart of the matter always proclaims this mystery of centrality. At the center of the atom, of humanity, of the earth, of the phenomenal world, and of the universe lies the Heart of existence from which radiates the pulse of life and from which irradiates the universe with its reality and light.

Two popular misconceptions in the contemporary worldview arise from our understanding of the functions of the two primary organs of the body, namely the brain and the heart. The first of these misconceptions lies in the assumption that the brain performs the highest function of the human being in its capacity to organize thoughts into a systematic whole and interpret their meaning in view of the contingencies of the outer environment. According to the traditional point of view, however, it is the heart rather than the brain that coordinates the activity of the various faculties and ultimately houses the mystery of the Transcendent Center. The brain resembles an elaborate and highly sophisticated machine—a computer if you will—that is able to coordinate millions of neural impulses per second in order to act, react, think through an idea, and come to a decision. However, from the point of view of the heart, it is spiritually inert and without that spark of life that can create and revolutionize inner worlds.

The second modern misconception lies in the popular attitude of the heart itself that functions primarily on a physiological level as the life-sustaining force of the corporeal system, as if the centrality of the heart and the vital functions of the person's inner aspirations could be reduced to the physical and chemical properties of a blood pump. On the contrary, if the brain and the heart were merely the primary and summative constituents of an inert and mindless matter, then we would be hard put as human beings to give a rightful accounting of ourselves as thinking beings with a consciousness that reaches beyond the known, physical world in order to embrace the truth of the metaphysical world. The physical heart is the consummate symbol of the inner heart; it is an outer manifestation with vital properties to the corporeal system, which reflects an inner sanctum with vital properties to the intellective and spiritual quality of the human being.

Beyond the horizon of the brain lie the mind, imagination, active thinking, and the self-reflective consciousness of the human being. All these faculties represent mysterious intangibles of the human entity that hover just beyond the edge of the physical brain as otherworldly phantoms of a netherworld whose resolution cannot be found within the neurons and protons of quantum physics or molecular matter. Beyond the horizon of the cardiac heart and in inverse relation to it lies the inner sanctum—what we refer to here as the "other heart"—that has virtually been forgotten by humanity during these times by virtue of the importance that has been invested in the brain—what the modern mind considers the faculty of intelligence together with the faculty of reason through which the intelligence can be expressed during these times. This other heart, the forgotten one, serves as the vital center of the inner being, its seat of intelligence and intellection, its niche of holy sentiments, the source of its affection and love, the repository and sanctuary of its inner self, and ultimately the faculty of synthesis, uniting through knowledge and love the totality of what we claim to be the humanity of our being.

The human heart establishes its signature and utters its truest word by being the symbol of humanity's spiritual center and the vertical axis upon which its knowledge and affection ascend heavenwards. As the symbolic image of humanity's true center, the physical heart lends its physiological meaning to the totality of the human being, but the force of its symbolic presence draws upon far deeper reserves within the vital essence of the human being. As such, the heart is the center not only of the bodily individuality, but also the center of the integral individuality, or the human being known and realized on both physical and spiritual modes of expression. When human beings become all heart, they express their inmost knowledge and feelings in such a way that the external world can witness the full range of their intelligence and sensibility.

Ironically, in today's world the heart that we now identify and remember as the seat of affection and sentimentality is actually the heart that forgets, while the other heart of our chapter title, the forgotten one, is actually the heart that remembers. The "heart that forgets" implies the absence of the knowledge and light that integrates the independent fragments of the human being into a synthesis of the Whole that is based on the unity and oneness of the Reality and the Supreme Identity projected into the universe by the Divinity. The other heart "that remembers" implies the presence of the knowledge and the light that illuminates the totality of the human being with the remembrance of our forgotten primordiality, when we walked with God, spoke with God, and knew God directly with a heart knowledge that knew no barriers or veils.

♣ ♣ ♣

Tradition relies on a number of images to qualify the heart's inner bearing, depending on the point of view envisioned and its role within the framework of particular human needs. The cave of the heart is a well-known traditional expression.[4] Within the Hindu tradition, the Sanskrit word *guha* means a cave, but it also means the inner cavity of the heart wherein the unconditional presence of *Atma* resides. The Chandogya Upanishad calls the heart the "seat of Brahma," a vital center with a small cavity in which the lotus can be discovered: "We must seek that which is in this place, and we shall know it" (8.1.1). As inner sanctum and "sanctuary without doors," the heart provides the inward, most hidden point in which *Atma* dwells, the crypt in which the inmost secret is preserved as the point of departure and final destination for all spiritual experience.

The Islamic tradition specifically refers to the heart as the seat of the intelligence,[5] which may be startling for a modern humanity imbued with the idea that intelligence resides in the brain as the vehicle of all conscious reckoning. The kind of intelligence referred to in this instance is one capable of pure intellection and not the kind of logical and discursive reasoning that the general public envisions when it makes reference to the word intelligence. As the seat, ground, and inner crypt (Greek: *kruptos*) of the intelligence, the heart symbolizes the sanctuary that fittingly provides the ambiance for an intelligence, not as we envision it today in its discursive and reflective modes alone, but rather in view of its far-reaching spiritual significance as a crystalline source of conscious awakening that reaches from the center of the mind and heart to

---

4. "The cave, or the grotto, represents the cavity of the heart considered as the center of the being" (René Guénon, *King of the World* [Ghent, NY: Sophia Perennis, 2001], p. 43).

5. The Greek philosophers, including Aristotle, also refer to the heart as the seat of the intelligence.

the Center of the universe and whose connecting golden thread is the acknowledgment of God and surrender to His Supreme Will.

In the traditional view, the heart does not merely serve as the embodiment of human affection and sentiment, a heart that corresponds to what the modern mentality believes to be the seat of affectivity, which amounts to being a source of heat for the emotions without the corresponding light that accompanies the knowledge of God. This concept of the heart corresponds to and complements the prevalent understanding of intelligence as the expression of a modern-day rationalism and nothing more. In spite of its rigid scientific approach to the understanding of a reality that finds its source—or rather proof—in physical matter, the modern mentality exhibits a curiously lopsided form of sentimentalism that considers the sentimental emotions to be the most profound expression of the human being. A purely sentimental heart, together with the rational intelligence prevalent among people today, has no patience with the view of the other heart found among people of more traditional cultures whose broad intelligence identifies with and draws its inspiration from the human intellect. Its intuitive insight cuts through the duality of this world with its direct perception of reality and transcends the narrow domain of human individuality by focusing on the knowledge of universal principles and higher realities.

The intellect, as the transcending faculty of higher sagacity and the human counterpart of the Universal Intellect, opens the human mind to the essential knowledge of God with its powers of intuitive and direct insight. As such, the intuition of God raises the human entity beyond the level of the purely human to experience the direct insight of the supra-human, permitting the mind a direct perception of the contents of the supreme light of the Universal Intellect through the mirror reflection of the human intellect. Now, according to the traditional view, this kind of intelligence finds its final abode within the human heart which, as the absolute center of the human being and the axis of vertical ascent, becomes the definitive point of contact between the human and the Divine. This direct perception of the knowledge of God and the truth of the One Reality is none other than what is sometimes referred to as heart-knowledge, a knowledge that is not always communicable, but one that can be experienced directly and fully internalized within the human being as a love that never dies.

The miracle of the intellect lies in the fact that it offers a knowledge of God that is direct and certain; that is to say, a knowledge that is perceived directly without signs, symbols, or veils and experienced with certitude, without any hesitancy, indecision, or doubt. It is perhaps both paradoxical and somewhat ironic that in spite of the assertive affirmation of this world that has resulted from the advances of modern science and the efficient pragmatism of the new technologies, the only thing that we do know for certain is the reality of our inmost being, our center and our heart, together with all that the heart implies within the framework of the human entity. Apart from the incontrovertible reality of birth and the harsh inevitability of death, and despite the onslaught of a multitude of outward impressions, the visibility of "things," and the purportedly objective presence of the physical and phenomenal world, the consciousness of our existence is the one absolute certainty that we treasure without any doubt.

A traditional irony and an existential paradox highlight the significance of what we wish to set forth. The traditional irony lies in the fact that the world and all its contents cannot contain the Divinity, but the heart of the true believer can contain Him, according to the well-known *hadith* of the Prophet Mohammed. As the microcosmic summative point of the universe and the symbolic image of the Divinity, the center of the human being reflects the Center of the universe whence originates and terminates all manifestation. The existential paradox lies in the fact that the inward reality that we cannot prove according to the criteria of modern science brings with it a feeling of certitude, while the physical body, the outer world of forms, and the entire external reality that we observe, quantify, and express through mathematical formulae to our heart's delight, evoke an air of unreality that is the direct result of their temporality, contingency, and ultimate finitude. In comparison with the Infinite and the Eternal, the manifested universe will always remain as good as nothing by way of comparison.

As deep cave and sacred crypt of the knowledge of God and prayer niche of the most profound human aspirations, the symbolic image of the heart focuses on the idea of a place deep within where something preternatural happens, where a realization of the numinous quality of life casts its glow across the field of our perceptions, where the knowledge of God burns as an inner flame and the presence of God is experienced in the heat of its afterglow. As the seat of the intelligence and the locus of centrality, the heart symbolizes an inner sanctum whose inward space offers a world without limits and a universe of infinite possibility. It is a sanctuary of knowledge tempered by feelings of love, a holy niche where our most sacred aspirations can be expressed and where an abiding intimacy with the Divinity can be experienced. As inner abode, the human heart is the place where the intelligence finds its home and where human intimacy with the Divinity makes itself felt as the ultimate expression of our relationship with the Highest Reality.

Beyond the concept of the heart as a locus of centrality and as a place where something not fully explicable happens lies the concept of the heart as an inward eye where some kind of witness sees with an inner vision, an organ of perception that has the capacity, indeed the prescience, of a conscious awakening that amounts to a vision of the one Reality. This inner eye of perception views with a lucidity what the external eye of observation and discrimination views with an opacity that recreates in the mind's eye the world of shadow-making. In its observation of the external, phenomenal world, the outer eye is able to experience a vision of God indirectly as it were through the signs and symbols of nature and through the spirit apparent in all living things. The inner eye of the heart, however, offers an alternative vision of the Divinity which is as direct and immediate as can be approximated within the human sphere of experience. As with the signs and symbols of nature, there is a unique harmony between the outer, opaque remembrance of God through the revelation of the phenomenal world, and the opalescent remembrance of God through the inner world of the heart.

The eye of the heart—the *'ayn al-qalb* of the Sufis—is the organ of inner vision and intuition of the knowledge of God. As such, it recalls the third eye and the eye of Shiva, the luminous eye of the heart and the eye of certainty (*'ayn al-yaqin*) that knows without any doubt what needs to be known and what can be known with certainty. The eye of the human heart is the reflection of the Eye of the Heart that is the non-manifested abode of the Supreme Being or the Universal Spirit, what Ananda Coomaraswamy calls, "a point without extension" or a "moment without duration," the Center and Axis of all existence, in which according to the Christian saint Bonaventura, "God's center is everywhere; His circumference nowhere."[6] The eye of the heart has featured in the traditional symbolism down through the ages. Before the Sufis, this same expression (*oculus cordis*) was used by St. Augustine when he wrote: "Our whole business therefore in this life is to restore to health the eye of the heart whereby God may be seen";[7] while Plato commented in his writings: "There is an eye of the soul which . . . is more precious by far than ten thousand bodily eyes, for by it alone is truth seen."[8] In the Gospels, the Sermon on the Mount still reminds modern humanity that the "pure of heart shall see God" (Matthew 5:8).

We have then a case for two visions within the borderland of the heart, the one external in order to view the world, the other internal in order to form the vision of a rarefied universe that intuits the knowledge of God and irradiates His presence throughout the macrocosm and within the microcosm of the human entity. "The eye by which I see God is the same eye by which he sees me," wrote the fourteenth-century mystic Meister Eckhart. "My eye and the eye of God are one eye, one vision, one knowledge, and one love."[9] And let us not forget to quote the American Transcendentalist Emerson who understood himself to be an organ of universal vision: "Standing on bare ground, my head bathed by the blithe air and uplifted into infinite space, all mean egotism vanishes. I become a transparent eyeball; I am nothing, I see all; the currents of the Universal Being circulate through me; I am part or parcel of God."[10]

As visionary organ of the senses as well as mediating symbol leading toward higher realities, the human eye enjoys various interesting modes of expression. Human beings have the capacity of vision, but what they actually see and how they see it depends as much on their inner as well as their outer eye. Human beings see the phenomenal world through the eyes of the body, their external vision; they see themselves and their fellows in interaction with the world through the eye of the mind—what we call the mind's eye—combined with the forces of memory, imagination, and insight; they see the inner world of the higher realities through the eye of the heart;

6. St. Bonaventura, *Itin. Mentis*, 5.
7. St. Augustine, quoted in E. F. Schumacher, *A Guide for the Perplexed*, p. 47.
8. Plato, *Republic* 527E.
9. Meister Eckhart, *German Sermon* 12.
10. Ralph Waldo Emerson, *Essays* (New York: Houghton and Mifflin, 1891), p. 147.

they perceive God directly as a vision of the Divinity with the eye of the intellect, which in turn reflects the Eye of the Intellect and the Eye of the Heart. Once again, Meister Eckhart: "Up noble soul. Put on your jumping shoes which are intellect and love."[11] Our intelligence and sacred emotions, in reflecting the eye of the human intellect, create a condition of knowing and experiencing that counterbalances the state of ignorance we would otherwise have to endure. The vision implicit in the human heart creates a condition of intelligent perception that intermingles with sacred sentiments, a knowing combined with feeling and sensibility that taken together create an internalized knowledge that ultimately reveals itself as the face of wisdom.

The heart is the container, the receptacle, the sacred repository that is ready to receive the light and the heat that accompanies the knowledge and love of God. The alchemy of the heart is a miraculous fusion of spiritual possibility and promise, a container whose contours already have the capacity of the Presence and are waiting to be filled with the knowledge and love of that sublime Presence. Unlike the heavens and the earth whose overwhelming magnitude cannot contain the Divinity, the "heart of My believing servant can contain Me" (*hadith*). In addition, God proclaims ominously in the Quran, "I am nearer to you than your jugular vein" (50:16), only to add in another verse on a more intimate level, "God cometh between a man and his own heart" (8:24). The heart substantiates the promise of transcendence within humanity that perceives and understands that God reserves the prerogative to enter the human heart because the heart has the capacity to receive the knowledge and contain the presence of God.

♣ ♣ ♣

The central message of the human heart is the knowledge of God and the one Reality that the Divinity encompasses. The central challenge of the human heart is the remembrance of God and its infusion into every thought, word, and action in order to create a living knowledge that unfolds within the life of an individual

---

11. Meister Eckhart, quoted in Chet Raymo, *Skeptics and True Believers* (New York: Walker and Co., 1998), p. 129.

through personal behavior and actions. This is a knowledge that concedes nothing to chance and leaves everything to the supreme wisdom of the Divinity, a knowledge that connects the human heart with the Universal Heart so that it is not the human heart but the Universal Heart that beats within the breast.

According to the prevailing worldview, modern humanity is identified as human primarily because of its brain power, including its supreme capacity to think, to reason, to self-reflect, and to inter-act with its surrounding world in a creative, discriminatory, and cog-nitive manner. Similarly, modern humanity, as a result of the untiring efforts of the modern scientific establishment and a com-prehensive secularist worldview that now invades every aspect of life, believes in a process of evolutionism, scientism, materialism and a form of progressivism that suggests that it is on a path that will ulti-mately lead to a perfection, a happiness, and a peace of mind and heart here on earth that will verify and bring to fruition the prevail-ing scientific concept of the human worldview.

Nothing could be further from the modern perception of humanity and its future potential than the traditional attitude toward the meaning of humanity, which does in fact promise perfec-tion, happiness, peace of mind and heart brought to fruition through a process, not of progress within the earthly condition, but ultimately a process of transcendence of self beyond the horizon of the human condition and beyond the dimension of this world as we know and experience it. According to the traditional perspective, humanity is distinctively human because of the true function of the heart as a faculty of synthesis in complement to the analytic faculty of the mind; a heart faculty with the supreme capacity to know intu-itively and instinctively, to desire that which is good, and to feel through higher levels of affection and intimacy a sacred emotion that is based on knowledge and that expresses itself as a love that reaches beyond the individual self toward the Universal Self.

Human intelligence contains knowledge of the Divine Being who embodies the Absolute Reality and the Universal Good. Intelligence thus envisioned leads to a profound desire and a deep aspiration on the part of humanity to partake of that knowledge and internalize it within as a defining truth. The natural consequence of the knowledge of God is the desire to achieve the promises of that knowledge, to realize the full potential of that reality, and to be good in view of the principial Good. When this state of mind and heart achieves a consciousness of these universal possibilities, "the kingdom of God" will then indeed be "within you" (Luke 17:21).

Human beings are vertical beings. Their thoughts, their desires, and their aspirations bespeak of an ascending desire to rise above themselves, to transcend their limitations, and to connect with the Intelligence, Consciousness, and Spirit that is evidenced in everything from the existence of a grain of sand to the procession of the galaxies. The Divine Being created a heart to serve humanity as its center and core. As center of the human system, the heart contains the knowledge of their primordial origin and final end, a first and ultimate knowledge that is the intuitive inheritance of the primordial heart, adequate to their spiritual needs and perfectly adapted to the vertical ascent. Because of the capacity of their heart, human beings can both know and communicate with the Divinity.

Heart-knowledge would be as nothing, however, without the higher consciousness that heart-knowledge activates. In approaching the meaning of higher consciousness, one can envision the cracking open of the universal egg and the spreading out of a subliminal and seminal "visionary awareness," a kind of ether of higher consciousness to wash over and permeate the entire concourse of the human mind and all its cognitive endeavors with this "esprit" of presence and the élan of higher awareness. Similarly, in conjuring up the symbolic image of the heart, we can envision a unique vessel whose contours are slowly filled with replenishment so miraculous and enriching that the heart becomes enlightened with the light of a pure knowledge and the warmth of an enduring love. It fills to brimming with the certitude of a universal knowledge, displays an incandescent clarity, and exudes a lenitive warmth whose afterglow is as intense and satisfying as the heat of a coal fire in a remote winter cabin.

At the inner boundary of the body is the mind, which is the faculty of direct outward perception. At the inner boundary of the mind is the heart, which is the faculty of direct inward perception. To phrase it differently, the heart is the isthmus between worlds, the one horizontal, three-dimensional, dispersed; the other vertical, multi-dimensional, and incisive. As such, one can speak of an outer and inner heart, just as one can speak of the outer and inner religion, this being in conformity with the two names of God in the

Quran, the Outwardly Manifest (*al-Zahir*) and the Inwardly Hidden (*al-Batin*). The heart is the center of the body in its outward capacity and the center of the human spirit in its inward capacity. On the outer level, it regulates the life-giving forces of the blood within the corporeal system; on the inner level, it is the faculty of direct spiritual awakening at the very threshold of the soul whose horizon implies a transcending arena that arrives ultimately at the very throne of God.

When God created Adam, He endowed his body with the rhythmic pulse of the heart and breathed into him the rhythmic breath of His Spirit, the drumming of the pulse and the expansion-contraction of the breath being the outward expression of an inner reality. The Divinity thus bestowed upon humanity two natural manifestations that were to be the major vehicles of knowledge on the one hand and of vitality on the other. The breath vivifies every cell within the corporeal frame, and the life functions of the body resound with the pendulous rhythm of the heartbeat. Thus, through the respiration of the breath and the pulse of the heart, the physical corpus becomes a living being.

What the breath does for the expansion and contraction of the Spirit of God within the living being, the heart does for the awareness of the Presence, providing the medium and the ambiance in which the Divinity may enter and take up residence. In addition to providing the vital life energy, what in the Hindu tradition is called *prana*, the breath establishes the rhythm of human respiration in which the expansion and contraction of the human breast reflect the great process of expansion and contraction that takes places on a cosmic scale within the universe and mirrors directly the two names of God in the Quran, namely, the Expander (*al-Basit*) and the Contractor (*al-Qabid*), symbolizing the cosmic principles of fullness and scarcity, growth and constriction, increase and decrease, that manifests in every aspect of the created world and that exemplifies the fundamental helplessness that lies at the root of existence without the abiding "Breath of the Compassionate."

The association of the breath with the heart coincides on a symbolic level with the relation of the breast with the heart. The heart is encased within the breast of humankind and like the heart the breast also conveys a symbolic meaning far beyond its purely physical reality. As the Quran says: "Is one whose breast God has expanded for surrender (*islam*), so that he has received enlightenment from God [no better than one hard-hearted]" (39:22)? Knowledge belongs to the fullness of the heart, but the Muslim's surrender to the reality of the one God belongs to the expansion of the breast. If the heart is expressive of knowledge and love, then the breast is the expression of an expansiveness that rises and subsides with the breath on the physical plane and expands and contracts with fear and hope on the inner plane. "Have We not expanded thy breast and removed a burden from you" (94:1-2) the Quran asks? The expansion of the breast opens the human breast/heart for the descent of spiritual insight. When Moses was sent to the court of Pharaoh, his immediate exclamation, according to the Quran, was: "Expand for me my breast" (20:25).

The breast is to the heart what the face is to the person, namely the face of the heart. In other words, the movement of the breast through the breath recollects the inner aspiration of the heart. The rise and fall of the human breast in response to the breath explicitly recalls a process of expansion and contraction that is symbolic of the process of denial of the truth and surrender to God that cuts to the core of the human self-image. Surrender represents an expansion of the heart, while denial of the divine possibility represents a constriction of the heart. Describing those whom God wishes to guide or lead astray, the Quran reveals: "He expands their breast to Islam. Those He wishes to lead astray, He constricts and closes their breast" (6:125). Ultimately, the symbolic imagery unites in the realization that the breath activates the remembrance of the heart to the extent that every breath becomes a remembrance of heart-knowledge. Both manifestations establish an inner rhythm of conscious vitality, the rhythm of the breath sustaining life and the rhythm of the pulse sending its vibratory drumbeat through the entire human system with the regularity of a metronome.

Modern science ignores the fact that humanity can conceive of things beyond the horizon of its mind, can desire to reach further than beyond, has a consciousness that is aware of itself, whose inner domain represents an objectivity and a certainty that leads ultimately to the higher archetypes that find their source and nourishment in the Divinity. Modern science is oblivious to or, even worse, deliberately ignores the fact that human beings can know themselves in ways other than through the purely empirical avenue of understanding. Modern science ignores the fact that the body without the soul does not constitute the human being and is no longer what is called a human person. It refuses to concede that human beings are made as a direct reflection of the Divine Prototype, exemplifying as they do all the qualities, attributes, and virtues that one usually associates with the Divinity and that within the tradition of Islam are identified through the ninety-nine names of God. Modern science ignores the fact that humanity has another heart, the forgotten one, in which God can dwell as a living presence and a truly felt reality.

At the heart of the human experience lies a fundamental mystery that virtually shapes and defines the way we experience the world. Similarly, at the heart of the universe lies a profound mystery that characterizes our understanding of the manifested universe and that challenges the human imagination to come to terms with the unknown quality of life. In other words, within the heart of both humanity and the world lies a veil that needs to be lifted and an isthmus that needs to be crossed, this being the fundamental challenge of the human experience. During the course of an individual life, the mystery begins to unfold, the formal meets the Formless, the thinking person meets the Universal Intellect, and sacred feeling meets the source of all intimacy in the knowledge and love of the Beloved.

The heart is to the human being what the Kaaba is to the religion of Islam: the point of departure for the vertical ascent heavenward and the heart pulse that energizes an inner movement that commences the ascension of hearts leading along the path of return whose goal is the transcendence of self as a prelude to union with the Divinity. In their role as earthly entities, human beings must remain something of a mystery to themselves, just as God exists in the eye of His mind and heart as the greater Mystery. Human beings must first come to know themselves before they can know their Lord.

If there is a secret to be revealed and if there is an essential knowledge to be unveiled and realized, then there must be an abode within the human being where this secret may lie hidden and where this knowledge may nurture and grow. There must be a faculty of perception that has the power of a mind, the depth of a heart, and the prescience of a spirit penetrating enough to crack open its protective shell in order to pour into the human being its overwhelming revelation with the steadfastness of the breath and the pulse.

That abode, that cave, that "kingdom of God within you," is the human heart, not the cardiac organ that beats soundingly within us, but the true heart that lies behind the symbolic image of humanity, in whose cavernous depths can be found our absolute center and the source of our vital being. This is the other heart of which we write, the one that remembers God and preserves Him within our lives as a living Reality and a conscious Presence. His remembrance resolves the mystery of the unknown, leads us across the lost continent of our inner being, and will bring us into the safe harbor of our future selves in the *vita venturi saeculi*, the life of the world to come.

Part Two

♣

Fields of Perception

Chapter Four

♣

Soul Instinct and Spiritual Imagination

Oh God, show us things as they are.
  (Prayer of Mohammed)

The very design of imagination is to domesticate us in another, a celestial nature.
  (Ralph Waldo Emerson)

Physically, mentally, and existentially, we stand at a point midway between two seemingly incompatible and alien worlds. This isthmus between worlds is none other than the borderland areas of the mind and spirit that separate the exterior world of the physical person and phenomenal nature from the interior world of mind, consciousness, soul, and spirit.

From the physical, mental, and existential points of view, human beings live in the world, take part in the innumerable experiences of the world, and are themselves a world within a world. Clearly, the exterior world is one that can be seen, felt, and directly experienced with the human senses because it is a tangible and visible physical reality. From the spiritual point of view, however, the world as experienced from the earthly point of view—with its physicality, its temporality, and its relativity—is but a prelude and first creation that will eventually defer and give way to a second creation that will directly reveal the unity and oneness of the true Reality whose parameters are metacosmic and whose spiritual compass constitutes the origin, source, center, and final end of all existence.

Because of the polarity that every man and woman must face regarding the existential nature of life, of existence, and of the manifested universe, all participate in a faith "of sorts," either consciously or unconsciously, willingly or unwillingly. Some people believe in the veracity of the world and in so doing unconsciously sustain a faith—however unwilling they may be to admit it—that this world, and the universe that envelops it, is what it appears to be, namely a living, breathing eco-system that has evolved over geologic and astronomical time into the apparent reality that it is today. Some people believe the human being to be the result of an evolution of purely physical and phenomenal processes that have passed through stages marking the transubstantiation of entire species eventually resulting in thinking, conscious human beings. On the other hand, some people consciously believe that the universe and everything in it, including the life force and conscious, reflective creatures, has been created by a Divine Creator, also referred to as a Supreme Intelligence, who will guide and sustain the universe throughout the course of its manifest destiny. Which one of these positions could be said to represent a knowledge based on faith and which a faith based on knowledge?

A fine line can be drawn between certain kinds of knowledge and faith, marking the difference between a revealed knowledge that grows into an enriching faith and a faith in a proposed—or desired—knowledge that has erected a precarious edifice whose foundation rests on a series of assumptions and suppositions about the world, which in turn relies for its substantiation on the world itself as the object of its inquiry. There is a ground to knowledge that needs to be identified and substantiated. In other words, the form and substance of a stated knowledge is not enough in and of itself; it must be substantiated in some way by identifying its first origin and primary source.[1] If a person proposes to know something, then the question must arise: whence comes this knowledge, from where does it derive its authenticity and how can its lasting value be truly established? This approach to the epistemology of knowledge has been predominantly ignored during these times and people, while they seem desperate to know about everything under the sun and pride themselves on any speck of knowledge they uncover, rarely question the knowledge they choose to believe in or the veracity of its origin and source.

The traditional point of view has always relied on a faith that is based on the descent of a revealed knowledge that passes through a

---

1. See the author's earlier work entitled *Near and Distant Horizons: The Question of Primary Sources and the Authenticity of Traditional Knowledge* (New York: Writers Club Press, 2000). "What are the sources of our knowledge and from whence does it derive its principial quality and its certitude? Are there headwaters for the laws and principles that flow through the cosmos into the mind of man? Is there a wellspring of knowledge that shrouds in a perennial mystery the origin of man and the birth of the universe and that seals with certainty the meaning and the ultimate fulfillment of man and the creation?" (p. xi).

prophetic messenger and finally arrives within the mind and mentality of a given civilization as a resolution to the mystery of origins and moves out into the world as a fundamental certitude of the truth of an Ultimate Reality. Firstly, faith begins to emerge within the mind as a quest for the genuine source of knowledge followed by the arrival of the knowledge itself, once the faith has been firmly implemented within the mentality of the mind as a conscious desire to believe. People living in a more traditional environment place their initial faith in the authenticity of revelation as the first source of knowledge, since as the absolute Word of God and not the relative thought of a human being, revelation is a direct communication from the Divine Intelligence to the human mind, identifying all the essential knowledge concerning the origin of the universe, of life, of humanity, and everything else that people need to know in order to lead their lives within the shadow of the truth and fulfill their destiny in the fullest expression of their true nature, their ultimate meaning, and their final end.

Within the normal course of our lives, we live on the surface of our being. Our immediate consciousness begins at the outer edges of a kind of operative unconsciousness, on the periphery of our selves, seeking always to project our individual egos outward into the world, to prove to ourselves that we exist and to be recognized as individual existences by the communities we live in. If we turn inward for a moment to the innermost sanctum of our being, beyond the inscrutable self, behind the intelligence that enlightens our minds, deep down into the well of our consciousness, and dig virtually into the ground of the human soul, a surprising revelation emerges to deliver its salient message back to the unsuspecting surface of the mind. There is, for want of a better term, a "soul instinct" within us that, upon inquiry, manifests itself as an invisible door that leads into a world of spiritual imagination and insight that is accessible, according to the well-known verse of the New Testament, to the person who knocks.[2]

Ever since aboriginal human beings first sat around the flames of a primitive campfire feeling provoked by the dark mystery that surrounded them, and ever since introspective human beings

2. "I tell you, ask and it will be given to you; knock and it will be open to you" (Luke 11:9).

painted scenes of animals in the darkness of mountain caves or buried their dead with funerary artifacts many millennia ago, humanity has felt an instinctive urge for the sacred, the numinous, and the mystery of being and becoming, ending finally in the sacred sentiment of reverential awe for the coming hour of the *mysterium tremendum*. It is a unique aspect of the human inheritance to extol the fundamental wonder of the world and the sense of the inexpressible that lies behind the phenomenal manifestations of the natural order. Human entities, as a matter of spiritual instinct, react to the awe-inspiring and universal *mysterium* that appears before them within the space-time continuum and touches their conscious mind with a vision of an alternative reality and a premonition of other worlds. The skin tingles, the hair stands on end, the heart pounds, and the blood stirs at the sight of a sunset in flames, a peal of thunder rumbling across the heavens, a bolt of lightening striking the earth, or the ghostly whisper of the wind through the trees. The body, mind, heart, and soul all react instinctively to the mystery that transcends the individual self and the natural world, representing a knowledge so powerful and an attraction so alluring that we are ready to give up the world and the self to behold and participate in its miraculous vision and drink down its saving nectar.

According to the various traditions, instinct is a non-reflective modality of intelligence, rather than the genetic inheritance formed in a purely cumulative and accidental manner which today's scientific community offers as an explanation for humanity's primitive, natural intelligence. Scientists now even refer to the identification and definition of epigenetic rules as the most effective way to make advances in the understanding of human nature. According to the various traditions, however, physical matter exists as a counterpoint to the world of the spirit to the extent that thinking finds its counterpart in neural activity and emotions find their substantive complement in molecular chemistry; but the physical world as the lowest order of reality could never serve as the evolutionary starting point for the higher human faculties. The traditional perspective identifies a spiritual instinct within us that initiates a knowledge, a faith, and a sacred sentiment representing a primary knowledge, an inspiring faith, and a spontaneous higher sentiment that reflects a first instinct of the soul as it responds to the contingencies of the existential reality and acts as a broadband receptive channel through which the impulses of the universal intelligence enters the world of the human mind.

Human beings believe in both seen and unseen nature and they take part in both seen and unseen realities because they have a spiritual instinct that opens an alternative door of perception. They are pragmatists on the one hand and mystics on the other. They would have disappeared long ago if they only believed in a world of dreams and a universe of precarious emotions. Instead, they have this instinct for faith that believes in a natural and observable world of reality whose forces they utilize in order to survive and they believe in a clarifying and inspiring world of the spirit whose forces they emulate in order to transcend the terrestrial world of imperfection and limitation.

When human beings observe the exquisite balance exhibited everywhere in nature, they feel a confirmation of what their instincts already know to be true. Only the law of God can have the ultimate claim upon their true allegiance and respect. No human law can approximate the spiritually instinctive attachment they have for the harmonizing and absolute law of God. Only a sacred law from Heaven can provide the balance and the equilibrium that human beings crave on the instinctive level, and only such a law can offer them the happiness that comes from an instinctive surrender and a willing conformity to the Will of God. Only a divinely revealed knowledge can provide the certitude that human beings need to substantiate their value system, their ethics, and their identity of self, and lead them in a direction that will ultimately bring them to their final destination and end.

The knowledge of primordial man and woman was directly accessible as a matter of existential and spiritual instinct. They not only enjoyed sight, but also a deep vision that allowed them to penetrate into the meaning behind the formal and manifested world of Nature. This inner eye of the heart plays a crucial role in humanity's understanding of itself and its role in the earthly sphere of existence. It is the eye of hope that ultimately offers a vision of certainty. The spiritual challenge of the traditional perspective for people living today is to reopen the eye of the heart, or to liberate human intelligence so that it can perceive once again the spiritual verities that were once second nature to primordial man and woman. As the fountainhead of this instinctive, primordial knowledge the first man and woman, and by spiritual inheritance the more traditional peoples of earlier times, drew upon their fundamental intuition of God, a spiritual instinct that pulls them ever inward toward the serenity and quietism that the inner life of the heart and soul promises.

There is nothing more forceful in human nature than the drive of human emotions. As untaught and non-reflective impulses, the higher emotions of fear, hope, and love emerge out of the human depths without a full accounting of their origin and source. A finger touches the pulse, a spark ignites, a door is unlocked and out marches a rarefied emotion and knowledge akin to the opening of a bud that has the capacity to transform minds and alter worlds with its direct access to an alternative reality. "The whole of existence frightens me," the philosopher Soren Kierkegaard is quoted as saying, "from the smallest fly to the mystery of the Incarnation, everything is unintelligible to me, most of all myself."[3] This instinctive fear of the unknown is counterbalanced in the 20th century by the implicit hope of the leading scientist of the modern era, Albert Einstein, who is quoted as saying: "A conviction akin to religious feeling of the rationality or intelligibility of the world lies behind all scientific work of a higher order."[4] We have here not the voice of great men quoting from ancient arcane philosophic tomes or philosophers and physicists playing on the shores of the universe or with the heart of the atom, but rather we have the voice of human instinct expressing the alternative sentiments of fear and hope that come forth as an irradiating quality whose certainty prefigures all temporal knowledge, all subjective thought and the empowerment of human beings to reason through the corridors of their cognitive thinking. An instinct for the numinous in life shines with its own light and cuts through the ignorance and contingency of the world like a flaming sword.

On the surface of life, we are never fully sure of ourselves. Certain questions linger in the background of our mind and occasionally raise their heads to the surface, only to sink back into the dark depths again to remain there in irresolution to reappear on another day. Do we look out onto the world with the cold indifference of a physical eye or is there a transparent eye within us whose

3. Soren Kierkegaard, quoted in Loren Eiseley, *The Star Thrower* (New York: Harcourt, Brace & Co., 1978), p. 190.
4. Albert Einstein, quoted in Loren Eiseley, *The Star Thrower*, p. 190.

perception and understanding makes a sacred niche of the world, in which everything is holy, reflects a knowledge of the Divinity, and is a symbolic remembrance of God. Despite the enormous immensity of the phenomenal universe, with its myriad stars and galaxies strewn across a vast heaven representing incalculable distances,[5] the world of space, time, and matter is not enough for us, not because it is not ostentatious enough, but because the immensity and implications of the universe are incalculable and leave us numb and cold in terms of their significance and meaning. We cannot adhere to a faith in its exclusive reality because we are not sure what it offers in and of itself. We sense on some instinctive level that we are not fully contained within its dimensions and that we extend somewhere else outside and beyond the physical continuum of the universe.

In fact, the species *Homo sapiens* represents the presence of a stranger in the prodigious void of lateral time and sidereal space since, even as a species of rational entities, they are totally negligible inside the purely existential reality. Within the inner world of instinct, intelligence, and higher sentiment, however, people are not strangers unto themselves but instead form a community of like-minded individuals in search of the fullest expression of their beings made possible through the gifts of the higher faculties. The inner reality is where we begin to find the makings of a true home to complement our deepest aspirations. Of course, we belong to the world in a manner of speaking by virtue of our existential reality. Our minds can apprehend electrons as well as the distant stars. We are made on the scale of the terrestrial mountains, oceans, and rivers. We reside on the surface of the earth and belong there, just as trees, plants, and animals do. But we also belong to another world: a world that is enclosed within us; a world that reaches beyond space and time; a world that represents a vast spiritual wilderness that needs to be explored in order to be fully realized; a world of spiritual imagination that makes possible our entrance onto the stage of the infinite.

5. We do not even realize it, but to gaze upon the night sky with the twinkling light of far distant galaxies is actually like looking into a vast archeological site of the universe. What we are witnessing is actually the residue of light that has traveled billions of light years to reach our casual glance and is therefore equally as old. To truly witness the momentality of the night sky would take another few billion years.

❧ ❧ ❧

Beyond the invisible door of soul instinct lies the broad field of the human imagination, a higher faculty that, like the other faculties we have been discussing in this work, has suffered from a profound narrowing of perspective and a dimming of vision during the modern era when it has been reduced to its lowest common denominator as a patchwork quilt of fantasy and idle dreams. In addition to being described as "the formation of a mental image that is neither perceived as real nor present to the senses," the stated meaning of imagination in today's dictionary also includes the following: "The ability to confront and deal with reality by using the creative power of the mind."[6] In Arabic, the term used is *'alam al-mithal.* There is also the Latin expression *mundus imaginalis* or alternatively the phrase *imaginatio vera,* which suggest an imaginative perception leading from the sensible to the suprasensible world, but the English word *imaginary* is clearly misleading in the modern context since what we commonly qualify as imaginary is dismissed as something that is unreal or phantasmal, reminiscent of the "madman's cornerstone" of Paracelsus,[7] rather than a faculty of perception that opens doors to a higher consciousness.

There is obviously some confusion and a divergence of opinion concerning the modern day understanding of the significance and meaning of the faculty of the imagination.[8] Is it a faculty of spiritual expansion and a window that opens onto the unseen reality as it is depicted in the traditional worldview, or is it the abode of the fantasy and habitat of a picturesque, imaginary, and ultimately false world whose fiction may be comforting to modern humanity but could hardly be identified as an authentic passageway into the realm of higher realities? Perhaps human imagination has gone the same way of the great myths of the world, which once represented inaccessible truths, but now suggest an arrant falsehood.

6. *The American Heritage Dictionary of the English Language* (3rd edition).
7. The ancient philosopher Paracelsus cautioned against the possible confusion between the notion of *imaginatio vera* and fantasy, what he called the "madman's cornerstone."
8. The French use the term *la folle du logis,* which literally means "the madwoman of the house."

Because the modern mentality does not admit of otherworldly possibilities and resides solely within a framework of perception in which everything—including human consciousness and the workings of the mind itself—can be reduced to the machinations of physical matter and neural impulses of the brain, there arises an inevitable problem of terminology in which spiritual concepts and terms lose their traditional flavor and no longer convey their primary meaning to a modern mentality long steeped within the bias of the physical world and the alleged objectivity of matter. This is not to say that the faculty of the imagination is no longer still highly valued by people today. On the contrary, the proliferation of fiction, fantasy, and the vast profusion of the film world, for example, amply testifies to the extensive influence that the imagination plays in cognitive thinking and creative living and the degree to which the mass audience of film-goers allow script-writers and directors to transfer the figments of their imagination into the minds of a gullible and bemused public.

Perhaps nothing heightens more the transitional world between body/soul and matter/spirit, and distinguishes the borderland between the spirit of the world and the world of the spirit than the world of the imagination, alternatively called in English the imaginal world (*mundus imaginalis*), which features in the traditional literature as an intermediary and mediatory place within the human mind and mentality that is actually a faculty and mode of perception for the higher realities. This intermediary universe, what the scholar of Islam, Henry Corbin, referred to as the "eighth climo,"[9] marks the isthmus between the sensory, phenomenal world of the earth within the grand phenomenon of the sidereal universe, and the supra-sensible world of the soul reflecting the supernal phenomenon of the vertical dimension with its direct and incontrovertible access to the intelligence, the heart, and the human intellect.

The imaginal faculty of perception constitutes its own integral world within humanity and possesses an imaginative power that combines the cognitive function of the mind with the noetic or spiritual value of the soul into an operative modality, which is as real as the perception of the senses and as vital to people's lives as

9. "The kingdom of 'subtle bodies,' the 'spiritual bodies'—threshold of the *Malakut* or the world of the *Soul*" (Henry Corbin, *On Imagination* [Ipswich, England: Golgonooza Press, 1976], p. 12).

intellectual intuition. This spiritual understanding of the faculty of imagination is virtually light-year's distant from the current usage of the term in which the *imaginary* is equated with that which is unreal, while the term *imaginal,* as in the imaginal world or the Latinate *mundus imaginalis,* is more in keeping with the spiritual connotation of the word. People today primarily equate their imagination with the powers of an inventive fantasy to conjure up pleasant images to soothe their restless minds; or they think of the kind of vivid imagination that highlights the creative aspect of the modern mind to come up with unusual or unexpected alternatives to the normal course of events as a means of escape. Still, there are vast differences between an inwardly directed, spiritual imagination and the aimless daydreaming and random, meaningless fantasies that merely allow people to drift on the surface of their somnolent consciousness.

Most people today highly value the play of their surface imagination without fully realizing its vast powers and the extent to which the imagination can bridge the gap that exists between the world of visual images and the world of eternal archetypes. In spite of the fact that a principal value of the modern world is the power of reason to solve the mysteries of the universe and the objectifying power of the senses to identify truth from falsehood, the modern mentality highly values the images, the dreams, the fantasies, the imaginings, and all the wild phantoms of its imagination that stir the mind, excite the desires, and fuel the dreams with a reality of their own making. This is the stuff of our subjective inner world, the product of our wishful thinking and a consequence of the poverty of a true spiritual imagination that participates in a *mundus imaginalis* and that therefore gives access to a broad range of metaphysical insight as a prelude to spiritual awareness.

In addition to the miracle of consciousness and the objective quality of the human intelligence, one of the powers that highlights our humanity and makes us human is the power to understand and process symbolic images through the power of the imagination. This power is not merely content to see the world as it appears to be and thus proclaim it as a given reality; it offers us a power over ourselves and the natural order by giving us the possibility of realizing a higher reality through the interaction of outer and inner worlds. Almost everything we ultimately do begins as a forethought in the mind's eye, which is none other than the richness of the higher imagination. All fears, hopes, and desires are envisioned, tested, and played out on the platform of the imagination before they ever come to life within the reality of our lives. Indeed, we may imagine the fruit of many lives within our imagination, even if we live only one true life. To imagine is the characteristic act not just of the mind of the poet, the painter, or the writer; it is a specifically human gift that is reflective of the minds of human beings generally, leading them into the future of themselves with inventiveness and creativity.

Needless to say, the existence of the faculty of the imagination as a mode of higher perception is a metaphysical necessity within the context of the spiritual world generally associated with the great religious traditions. It makes possible the journey of return *ab extra ad intra*, the journey to the eighth clime from the external world of the senses to the internal world of the spirit. The world of the senses and the cognitive world of the mind provide the basis for processing the world we live in, while the world of the spiritually active imagination serves as the bridge between the lower world of the senses in interaction with the rational mind and the purely intelligible and archetypal world of the spiritual realities in interaction with the intellect.

For one thing, spiritual imagination allows human beings to imagine the reality of higher spiritual experience that occurs during prayer and meditation and that serves as a prelude to direct spiritual experience. In addition, they can perceive the veracity and truth of the spiritual meaning of revelation on the one hand and the symbolic and revelatory messages of the natural order on the other as an initial perception of imagination, leading a person beyond the limited mindset of matter and mind typified by the purely rational mind into higher levels of thinking and perception. As such within the traditional perspective, the imagination serves as an organ of receptivity of a higher knowledge as does the intelligence, with cognitive and perceptive powers of the highest order that amply assist human beings in their quest for a truer understanding of the reality in which they live.

For the modern individual living in the contemporary world, the journey to the eighth clime, to the lost land of a higher perception and to an imaginal world that employs the power of a

spiritually charged and heightened imagination, to cross boundaries and transcend worlds is a journey that will never begin. Such
a journey beyond the lower realm of sense perception and rational
thinking into the higher realms of spiritual and imaginal perception requires a brave commitment to a concept and vision of the
Whole that draws its reality and its truth from the first Origin and
the original Source found only in the various revelations of the
great world religions.

It may seem imaginary, for want of a better word, to the modern
mentality to think that it is possible to leave the world of the senses
and the objective world of matter without leaving reality itself. On
the contrary, leaving the sensible world behind connotes, in the first
instance, a distancing from the sensible world of matter for the sake
of the immanent reality of the spiritual order as the one and only
enduring reality that can truly respond to the needs and the inmost
desires of a person. The sensible world is perceived in this instance
as the world of subjectivity, being the product of the mind, reason,
and senses and thus a figment of the imagination; while the imaginal world is perceived as a participation in a world of objectivity that
finds its ground in the intellect, intelligence, and imagination as the
basis for spiritual experience.

♣ ♣ ♣

The modern-day approach to studying the phenomena of the natural and cosmic order betrays a fundamental failure of the contemporary imagination to apprehend what is at stake in the pursuit of
knowledge and the search for an understanding of the true nature
of reality. Nowadays, we tend to regard our imagination as an inventive faculty working on its own and in isolation, independent not
only of our reason but of the spiritual intellect as well.

On the one hand, within the well-specified context of the modern scientific worldview, we have the embedded attitude that matter
is objective and therefore real, based on what the senses can verify.
It does not seem to be a concern that quantum physics has proved
the illusion of this by reducing the substance of matter to such a
degree that it no longer exists in the solid state, resulting in the discovery that subatomic particles are no longer the basic building
blocks as envisioned first by Democritus and later Newton. They are

only idealizations that are useful from a practical point of view to make predictions, but that have no fundamental significance.[10]

On the other hand, we have the traditional attitude that all natural phenomena, all objects in creation, and virtually all matter has a sacred quality in addition to its purely physical quality. The physical world bears within its particular form the essence of a *logos* and a revelation that fulfills the promise of its latent energy. In other words, the world, the universe, indeed the cosmos is virtually sacred in light of its creation by a Divine Being. It carries within its matter and form the seeds of a divinity and a sacredness that is the counterbalance to the physicality of its form. Its sacrality, however, cannot be realized or fulfilled, in a manner of speaking, without the interiorizing consciousness and spiritual imagination of the human being. Objects are not what they are claimed to be by modern science; but they would remain remote, cold, and distant in their sacrality without the perception, the imagination, and the spiritual insight of humanity. "It is in and through us that the physical world is hallowed and that its intrinsic sacramental quality is revealed."[11] If the world is a revelation of God, then the mind with its accompanying faculties is the organ through which this revelation is witnessed and experienced. The vast potential of phenomenal nature is actualized and ultimately realized through the perception of the human mind.

It is also the faculty of human imagination that processes images, signs, and symbols from the pictograms that they are on the surface of reality into the symbolic meaning they secretly preserve within their form. The natural images of today are no longer symbols whose form contains an inner meaning. The universal symbol makes possible the concomitance of the visible and the invisible, the earthly with the sublime, physical form with spiritual meaning. As such, they also contain within themselves the force of revelation and the power to bring down and make available to the human mind, indeed the human imagination, the knowledge of

---

10. In the words of famed physicist Niels Bohr: "Isolated material particles are abstractions, their properties being definable and observable only through their interaction with other systems" (*Atomic Physics and the Description of Nature* [New York: The Macmillan Company, 1934], p. 57).
11. Phillip Sherrard, *The Sacred in Life and Art* (Ipswich, England: Golgonooza Press, 1990), p. 12.

the archetypes and of the intrinsic sacredness of all created forms within nature.

Similarly, in the Islamic perspective, the acquisition of knowledge and the internalization of forms that are perceived by the outer senses is made possible through the unique capacity of the imagination. Reflection upon the role of the imagination as a human faculty features highly in the metaphysics of Ibn al-'Arabi. He writes: "God made imagination a light through which the assumption of forms by all things . . . may be perceived. Its light penetrates into sheer nonexistence and gives it the form of an existence."[12] This manner of understanding the true nature of human imagination may seem alien and exaggerated to the modern mentality, but it will seem far less extreme, if not even more appropriate, if one understands the meaning of the spiritual imagination as he envisioned it to be.

The traditional point of view maintains that the imagination is an organ of the soul and a subjective mode of perception for the higher realities. The vision of the soul is actually created initially by the spiritual imagination in its capacity as a human organ of perception that is in harmony with the divine imagination: the human mind meeting the Mind of God with open inquiry and the Mind of God meeting the human mind with revelatory knowledge in compensation. For example, in the dream state in which the imagination plays a major role, dream images are perceived in a sensory form, yet they are vivified by a consciousness that is actually a heightened awareness which serves as a channel for supra-sensible realities. In dreams, sensory objects from the outside world take on a kind of spiritual nature within the never-never land of dreams in which the inanimate matter of the corporeal world and the living and luminous substance of the spirit come together, thus spiritualizing the material world, just as the imagination has the capacity to materialize the spiritual world in our everyday encounters with life.

In this way, the faculty of the imagination serves as the isthmus or borderland through which the divine essences of things are brought down into their corresponding exterior forms, and through which the exterior, physical forms of things are spiritual-

12. William C. Chittick, *The Sufi Path of Knowledge* (Albany, NY: SUNY Press, 1989), pp. 122-123.

ized and made holy. "It is a specific power of the soul that builds bridges between the spiritual and the corporeal. On the one hand, it 'spiritualizes' corporeal things that are perceived by the senses and stores them in memory. On the other, it 'corporealizes' the spiritual things known in the heart by giving them shape and form. The soul's 'storehouse of imagination' (*khizanat al- khayal*) is full of images derived from both the outward and the inward worlds."[13] Spirit comes down and enters the body so that the body may be vivified and become as spirit.[14]

Imagination also plays a major role in the understanding and perception of the words of revelation. Prior to receiving the initial revelation, the Prophet of Islam experienced some very powerful inward signs while meditating in a cave on the outskirts of Mecca. He spoke of "true visions and when asked about them, he said that they were like 'the breaking of the light of dawn.'"[15] In its intermediary and mediatory role, the spiritual imagination is able to take the objective configuration of reality as presented in scriptural revelation and process it in such a way that it becomes a subjective reality within the mind and an operative factor as a mode of perception. Objectively, imagination relates to the principles and truths of the divine disclosure of the Word of God, while subjectively it internalizes the revealed knowledge of God within the mind, heart, and ultimately the soul of the human being. It becomes the soul's outlet into the world and the world's inlet into the soul, spiritualizing the phenomena of the world by perceiving them for what they are in their essence.

During the modern era and since time immemorial, much of what people have believed has used the imagination to give it shape and form. Whether one chooses to use the imagination as a vehicle of the imaginary in its modern connotation, of image-making and of fantasy, or to raise the stakes and lift the mind's capacity to perceive and process the higher verities, perhaps that in itself takes a kind of imagination that modern humanity is unwilling to participate in.

---

13. William C. Chittick, *Imaginal Worlds* (Albany, NY: SUNY Press, 1994), pp. 71-72.
14. "'Behold!' The Lord said to the angels: 'I am about to create man, from sounding clay from mud molded into shape. When I have fashioned him and breathed into him of My spirit, fall ye down in obeisance unto him'" (Quran 15:28-29).
15. Martin Lings, *Mohammed: His Life Based on the Earliest Sources* (Kuala Lumpur, Malaysia: Noordeen, 1983), p. 43.

For what, in the end, do we imagine in the dark night of our unknowing but the essential—indeed the crucial—question of our collective, mysterious origins, the origin of life, the origin of the universe, the final explanation and the last word that would unite the universe into a unified theory of reality that could no longer be impertinently questioned or doubted. In the final analysis, it is not God that we imagine, for that is impossible, being beyond the limited range of the human mind. Instead, we imagine the significance of God in every tree, river, and mountain in our field of vision, and the consequences of God in every thought, every emotion, and every future desire within the consciousness of the mind.

In addition, it should be asked: What requires imagination? The answer, more difficult now than ever before, lies in the encounter with life itself: none other than to live a life wisely and well. To live life wisely means to acknowledge a body of knowledge from a legitimate and authentic source, a higher source than anything we can imagine on our own, and to apply this knowledge as an overlay of the mind in the pursuit of one's thoughts and decision-making, in one's behavior and in one's actions.

To live a life well means to shed the dark impulses of the soul as a snake sheds its skin for the sheen and luminosity of the virtues and the beatitude implicit in the stations of wisdom. It is to see within the inanimate phenomena of nature an animate presence, a *logos* and a revelation that reflects the knowledge of a higher reality and that serves as a symbol for a greater truth. It is to feel within the heart the knowledge of God as the love of God and to preserve the sole overriding desire to unite with that Reality. It is to look into the mirror of the self and see, not the ancestral image of a humanoid or an ape, but the reflection of the primordial and Adamic man whose intelligence was intuitive and direct, and whose sentiments were heart-felt and full of love for the Supreme Being, for such was the ancestral Adam that he was the friend of God and His representative on earth.

How human beings choose to exercise their imagination and the extent to which they allow themselves the luxury of full reign over its range and vision lies within their own power to initiate and bring to the surface of their mind. A man or woman has faith and believes in God, not out of naiveté, or terror, or some psychological void of mind and heart in search of a comforting response to the mystery of life, but rather as a consequence of a fundamental instinct for the essential and for the supernatural, what we have referred to here as an instinct of soul that is unique and that expresses itself every day of our lives through the forces of higher imagination.

As human beings, we live within a world of nature that we pretend to know, only to realize, through our imagination in its highest manifestation, that we stand at the doorway to the infinite, to a world beyond nature that we do not know and cannot experience directly. We see our own shadow emerge from our footsteps; we hear the voice of conscience whisper the wisdom of an abiding truth; we feel the force of the spirit as "the wind that bloweth where it listeth, and thou hearest the sound thereof but canst not tell whence it cometh and whither it goeth."[16] At such moments, an uncanny feeling emerges from the shadow of the mind that an invisible doorway has suddenly been opened that, widening out, leads us beyond the person we know ourselves to be, in order to meet the person we have the potential to become.

Imagine how it would be, to have the beginning and the end and all that passes in-between existing within our beings as a principial reality? What would it really mean to fully realize the Quranic truth that "wherever you turn, there is the Face of God" (2:115)? The imagination begins in the mind as a modality of creative inquiry and ends by becoming a threshold to the spiritual realities, so that we can be shown and see things as they are and become the true beings that we were intended to be.

---

16. The words of Christ to Nicodemus (John 3:8).

Chapter Five

♣

Inside the Niche of Higher Emotions

"What a man loves a man is."[1] If he loves a stone he is that stone, if he loves
a man he is that man, if he loves God—nay, I durst not say more; were I to
say, he is God, ye might stone me. I do but teach you the scriptures.
    (Meister Eckhart)

The primary dogma of modern science is that reality can only be
ascertained through the objectivity of matter and the objectifying
quality of human reason, whose mandate is to navigate its way
through the enigmas of the world and to identify through the observation of the senses the truth and the ultimate reality of the universe.
Now if we were to believe and fully accept this infernal message, how
could we account for the wealth of emotions and feelings that com-
prise the vast, inner world of human consciousness and holy sentiment. This world necessarily includes the world of our imagination
and the full range of our creative life: the realm of dreams and the
activity of the human psyche with its unconscious desires and sub-sur-
face urges, the knowledge and sentiment of an affective heart, and
the grounding essence of the human soul where the existential battle
of the self is fought—the greater *jihad* according to the Prophet
Mohammed—between the opposing forces of our inner nature.

    A deep, existential chasm exists between what the modern scien-
tific worldview proclaims to be true—but that ultimately may prove
to be mere fictions of the mind—and certain figments of the imagination that lie outside the realm of scientific observation and yet
have an air of truth about them to the extent that they are universally accepted as serious witnesses of what we perceive to be a valid
and true aspect of reality. It is one thing to desire to understand the
world from the empirical point of view; but that desire should not
preclude the possibility of looking at the world and taking into
account the sense of awe and wonder which is a part of humanity's
primordial heritage when everything in the phenomenal world of

1. St. Augustine, *Confessions.*

89

nature radiated outward with a halo of inner vitality and meaning, before the world had "solidified" into a purely outward form and veiled the direct vision of the animating spirit.

Of special significance within this context is the role played by human feelings, emotions, and sentiments whose impression of reality cannot be denied because they are felt and experienced by virtually every human being on the planet. Like the elusive quality of the heart and soul, somewhere within each individual lies the region of the emotions. We are aware that these emotions exist because we experience them in our lives so often and so profoundly. They happen and make their presence felt, forming shadows of a truth within the soul that cannot be denied. The poignancy of their expression affects every experience in our lives and they exert a profound influence over our minds, our understanding, and our consciousness generally. In addition, true emotions and sacred sentiments reach beyond the ordinary level of human experience and touch the mainstream of human lives with the wand of stardust. In a single stroke of feeling, a window of perception briefly opens whose magical power reminds people of the dark, mysterious field of their celestial origins and has the visionary foresight to project people on the course that will lead them to their true destination.

The fact remains that the human mind with all its multi-faceted layers of perception is not enough for human beings, for the simple reason that the knowledge which is the end-product and final outcome of their mind may show them where they need to go, but will not actually bring them there without the sentiment and love and driving will power to lead the way. The world of essential knowledge, as an objective modality, is intimately connected with our intelligence and the intellect that make such knowledge accessible to the mind. The world of our emotions, as a subjective modality, is intimately connected with our will and our desire to put into action within the human world that which we know to be true. The road back to the Garden that we are promised passes through the heart of the human being and not the mind. The affective heart and not the cognitive mind will lead us back out of the world and toward the transcendent Intellect through holy sentiments and sacred emotions that are based on the knowledge of God.

Every human being possesses a sacred niche that serves as the point of departure and focus for all sacred sentiment. In Islam the outer prayer niche is the *mihrab* in a mosque where the *imam* stands in order to lead the ritual prayer, which indicates the ritual orientation toward Mecca. The inner prayer niche is the symbolic and summative point within the mosque enclosure that symbolically gathers together and embodies all of the prayers and holy aspirations of the faithful, sending forth their aspirations horizontally in the direction of Mecca, before ascending vertically toward the celestial heights that transcend the three-dimensional world of humanity. The prayer niche contains the solitary voice of our deepest and most heart-felt sacred emotions. It is the focus of intimacy between the creature and the Creator and the axis upon which arises the sacred relationship between the human and the Divine. The God of our mind develops and takes shape within us according to the open gate of the intellect and the extent of our conscious awareness at any given moment through the discerning force of the intelligence. The God of our heart fuses the *knowledge* of what we know to be true with the *experience* of what we know to have felt.

The God of the mind is one experience of the Divinity; the God of the heart is another. They meet in the soul where human self-hood finds its fullest and most complete expression. It is the human spirit in the form of a soul that lays ultimate claim to the accomplishments of a human life. Human beings have had no part in the arrival of the animating spirit; but with its coming, *Homo sapiens*, the ethical animal, found within a light that no other animal ever had before, a light that modern science simply cannot account for and will never classify on its own terms. Traced back through the history of time, the human soul simply disappears into the antediluvian woods with the traces of its footsteps.

Nothing responds more movingly and more whole-heartedly to the secret within humanity, to the enigmas of the universe and to the mystery implicit in the idea of a Supreme Being, than the broad range of experience that constitutes the inner life of human affections. A clear distinction needs to be made at the outset between sacred sentiment and higher emotion as portrayed in the great world religions, and the emotionalism or sentimentality so prevalent in today's world, which seems to have come into the forefront of human consciousness as a compensation for the lack of the true higher emotions that traditional people expressed in response to their sense of the Divinity. Human sentiment is an open door to a higher world of knowledge and experience in the light of a revelation of the objective reality and permits people to experience the world as a process of assimilation in which the best of the world passes through the best of the individual on the way to the revelation of the inner self. Emotionalism-cum-sentimentality, on the other hand, is a purely subjective condition, such as a passing mood or preference, which can distort as much as it absorbs, and where the inward and purely individual condition of a given soul in the form of an ego becomes an obstacle to a true awareness of realities both within and beyond the world.

In referring to the human emotions and sentiments, we do not mean the lower emotions that frequent the passageways of the human psyche or the romantic and affected sentiments that have come to be the defining experience of modern, humanistic life. At best, these mundane emotions help moderate the vast wealth of impressions that people must deal with in their daily life and channel those feelings into a comprehensible mode of expression. At worst, these elemental sentimentalities come to be understood as the most profound and elevated expression of the modern psyche, offering up the heat and perhaps inner turmoil of the moment without the supporting light of the intelligence. Instead, we are referring to the higher emotions and the sacred sentiments that combine the most enlightened aspects of knowledge with the highest and most substantive modes of feeling of which the human being is capable, and that virtually define the nature of the spiritual experience. In the words of Frithjof Schuon: "Knowledge is beyond sentiments; but sentiments can be modes of indirect knowledge, according to the reality of their content."[2]

People living in more traditional times witnessed this mystery of God everywhere, in keeping with the Quranic verse: "Wherever you turn, there is the Face of God" (2:115). From the existence of a grain of sand to the sublime procession of the celestial galaxies spread across the night sky, God is witnessed as the "Creator of the heavens and the earth" (14:19). Because more traditional people acknowledged the rare ability of the unknown quality within phenomenal nature to lure the human psyche out of itself and tempt it

2. Frithjof Schuon, *Logic and Transcendence* (New York: Harper Torchbooks, 1975), p. 163.

beyond its limited perspective, they were able to respond with a full spectrum of emotions ranging from curiosity to interest to awe to reverence to a profound fear and a far-reaching love of the Sublime that they saw evidenced throughout the natural order of the universe. Nothing stirs the human emotions more fully than the astonishing miracles of ubiquitous Nature, capitalized here to encompass the full manifestation of the phenomenal world in memory of what was once referred to as Mother Nature. Its perennial mystery, its savage wildness, its innocent quality of enchantment, and its revelatory messages have permitted people of earlier and more traditional times to come to an understanding of themselves and their surroundings in such a way that they could combine the knowledge embedded within the phenomena of symbolic nature with the sacred emotions and holy sentiments that symbolic nature inevitably arouses within the human heart.

On fundamental levels, human beings are first of all animals. They are by-pedal animals that walk upright, which only makes them resemble a human being. They are cognitive animals, but that only makes them modern human beings. Human beings are at heart emotional animals. We write "at heart emotional" because the best of humanity always emerges from the sentiments of the heart rather than from the machinations of the brain. To say that human beings are at heart emotional beings is to unravel all the contingency surrounding them to arrive at their absolute core in order to discover the very source of all that they are within their center.

What do we find when we arrive at the heart of the human nucleus if not a person whose superior knowledge and self-awareness come together and merge with the unique forces of higher emotions and sentiments that are a uniquely human characteristic, forces that have the power to transform the person into a high level spiritual being—a virtual *Homo spiritualis*—a person with the capacity to transcend the limitations of their being and ultimately perfect themselves. People react instinctively to the force of thunder because its thunderous sound moves them emotively with fear and awe and reminds them of the voice of God. They listen to the ghostly sound of the desert wind and remember the eerie feeling of a ghostly spirit. They perform a symbolic gesture such as the hand over the heart or the bowed head to convey a holy sentiment. They hear the echo of other worlds in a seashell; their minds discover the atom in the universe, while their heart imagines a universe in an atom. Human beings have never lost their ability to feel, whether it be from the depths of their being to express a yearning and a premonition to reach beyond the individual self for the Greater Self, or the simple, sympathetic empathy for a bird with a broken wing. Through the best of their emotions, they willingly offer the best of themselves to other people because their self-offering substantiates and summarizes all that a person knows and feels into a solitary expression of pure love.

In Part One of this work, we discussed the significance of the intelligence and the luminous source of its discernment and insight. We mentioned the variety and levels of perception and pointed out that humanity's intelligence becomes manifest and shows its true face in its thinking, decision-making, and behavior through actions and works, thereby serving as a bridge within the borderland of the spirit between the contingency of this world and the ethereality of the other side of reality. If ignorance has a dark side and a bold face, then human intelligence has an illuminating aspect and a subtle face, showing shades and colors of shadow and light that reflect the level and station of a person within the hierarchy of being and the extent that they are connected with the knowledge that has been absorbed from the intellect.

Human sentiment, on the other hand, represents another modality of perception. Sentiment is not knowledge precisely, although it contains knowledge within the fullness of its expression, and it is not precisely a manifestation of free will either, although it contains a force whose source can be found within that will. How, then, are we to envision the true significance of human sentiment? What is its actual role within the repertoire of human faculties and modes of perception and what exactly is it seeking to accomplish in this world?

In a manner of speaking, human sentiment could be likened to the first layer of the soul or the open face of the soul to the world. If the soul is the ground and bedrock of the individual entity, the true composite of the human being's essence and the summary of the inner person, then the emotive sensibility comprises the first layer of earth in the ground of the soul where the initial yearning for the greater Self takes root. The higher sentiments of compassion, generosity, charity and the corresponding virtues all lead a person out of and beyond the individual self in a translation of creative thought to higher emotion that ultimately becomes a love of the Divinity and the desire for union with the Beloved. The process may be the adoration of the Sovereign Good and the final goal may be union with the Sovereign Being, but its heart-felt reverberation begins with the initial experiences of higher emotions and holy sentiments as they are felt within the human being and as their effect extends out into the world.

True knowledge, in particular any knowledge associated with the principial knowledge of God, is objective, discerning, and contemplative. As such, it is the expression of an intellectual reality that is definitive and absolute. Sentiment, on the other hand, is emotive rather than discursive and is the human expression of an emotional subjectivity that arises within the human being as an existential reality to the extent that the emotions exist, are truly felt, and therefore cannot be denied. Sentiment takes the knowledge of God and internalizes it within us as a subjective reality that can first be experienced as a prelude to becoming fully internalized. As such, it is the expression of an emotional reality that is simple, direct, spontaneous, freely expressed and genuinely felt.

Knowledge serves as a kind of internal skeleton within the emotive vista of the human being. It provides the skull and bones of our understanding of ourselves and our surrounding world and permits us the luxury of placing ourselves and our world within a universal framework that has meaning and makes sense. The corresponding sentiments and emotions that arise and are taken on by us as a result of the revelatory and essential knowledge of God also act as the flesh and blood of the internal noetic system, the substantive heat and life force of a knowledge that allows us to be ourselves and leads us toward the future of our manifest destiny.

Human intelligence, free will, and holy sentiment represent individual worlds that interact and ultimately unite within humanity to create a spiritual dimension that serves as an essential component in understanding the true nature of the human being and the universe. The intelligence contains the knowledge of God and this then generates desire. Thereupon, free will inspires the mind to act on behalf of its intelligence and evokes the feelings of higher sentiment. The emotions then awaken the inner being to the possibility of a departure from the closed system of the individual ego and beyond the edge of knowledge for the sake of an experience of supreme awakening as a prelude to union with the Divinity.

♣ ♣ ♣

As the universal first principles of all human endeavors, principial knowledge and higher sentiment serve first and foremost to accomplish union with the Divinity. The purpose of knowledge is union through intellection and insight and the purpose of sentiment is union through aspiration and love. Their objective is the same, but their manner of expression and modality of approach are different. One is the path of a universal knowledge which synthesizes the entire body of the cognitive, intellective, and discriminatory fields of vision within a framework of objectivity based upon the revelation of the Absolute Being; the other is the path of human love which, as the summative and quintessential expression of the higher emotions, summarizes the sentient, affective, and emotive fields of vision within a framework of subjectivity based upon the human revelation in view of the Beloved. Curiously enough, these two paths exist within us and configure our spiritual effort with a blessed combination of knowledge and love. Knowledge without love would be like a principle without its complementary action. Love without knowledge would be a reaction and a consequence without its first principle and primal cause. Together, they steer the course of our inner life to its final resolution in "the one thing needful," namely unity with the Divinity.

We cannot expect to live effectively in the world without the sacred emotions that the heart offers and we cannot expect to understand the world without the knowledge that life demands. Indeed, who in their right mind would even want to? for that would be tantamount to preferring the eternally frigid darkness of the night sky to the rich warm blue of the vault of the heavens. Certainly, the vast dome of the empyrean, with its flash of eternal blue spread across the daytime sky, summons otherworldly instincts and holy emotions that are drawn into the profound depths of humanity through feelings of wonder, mystery, and awe. The blue firmament recreates in one striking, symbolic stroke the primordial paradise that lies within the inner landscape of humanity as a latent memory and potentially future reality. The eerie panorama of the night sky, on the other hand, with its plate of eternal darkness accented by the cold light of distant stars, without the symbolic knowledge that must accompany such a universal image, contains no comprehensible message that can relate to humanity's immediate experience and harbors no human feeling that could be recognized within that cimmerian,[3] icy, and silent void. As a sacred and symbolic architecture, the dome of heaven contains for us the message of darkness and light, the message of light serving as the perennial remembrance of the knowledge of God and the message of darkness serving as the perennial warning of the absence of the Divine Presence, amounting to the hopelessness and chaos that characterizes the supreme alienation of the damned.

Principial knowledge combined with human sentiment is therefore vital to human beings. *Homo sapiens* would have disappeared long ago if they had persisted in living in a world of dreams rather than known realities and in a universe of precarious moods and whims rather than the higher emotions and sacred sentiments that characterize the defining quality of their humanity. More traditional societies than today's pursued their life in a world of reality that was revealed, natural, observable, symbolic and thus meaningful, a world in which they existed and whose forces they used in order to survive; but they lived that life by virtue of an inner field of perception whose higher emotions and holy sentiments permitted them to understand the objectivity of their knowledge through the subjective experience of their own being. A melody is built on the foundation of notes, instruments, and the hands or breath of the person who creates it, but the temper of the soul awakens these facts of music to another level of experience and allows a person to perceive inwardly the spirit of the music. The blue color of the sky or the arrangement of musical notes represent a configuration of facts and figures that mysteriously leave an impression on the mind that the technical facts alone cannot begin to approximate.

Emotion exists as a complement to human intelligence and the powers of discernment, and not as a sentimental and subjective burden clouding the reality of the moment. Therefore, feelings are important in coming to terms, not only with the objective world in which we live, but also in understanding and interiorizing the principles of metaphysics that overlay all of existence. While these principles of knowledge may appear in many instances to be purely

3. A people from Greek mythology described by Homer as inhabiting a land of perpetual darkness.

abstract and remote, they in fact have the power to confer upon the soul feelings of certitude, serenity, peace, and joy as a complement to the substance, the knowledge, and the meaning of a given truth. These sentiments serve as modes of perception that can actually deepen our comprehension of truth and lead in turn to the practice and development of the virtues.

> To say that man is endowed with sentiment capable of objectivity means that he possesses a subjectivity not closed in on itself, but open unto others and unto Heaven; in fact, every normal man may find himself in a situation where he will spontaneously manifest the human capacity for compassion or generosity, and every man is endowed, in his substance, with what could be called the "religious instinct."[4]

Knowledge leads down the path toward wisdom; but generosity, compassion, love and the other higher emotions lead down the path toward virtue.

♣ ♣ ♣

The need for specificity and the desire to set forth appropriate examples require that we forthwith enter the real world of human sentiments and higher emotions in order to express in words what is normally only felt within. The list should be long and comprehensive, but space requires that we be focused and succinct. We will therefore briefly discuss a number of primary, principal sentiments that amount to a mosaic of contradictory feelings, emotions, and sacred aspirations that form the backcloth of the human soul and spirit:

- · HUNGER AND DESIRE
- · DESPAIR AND HOPE
- · FEAR AND REVERENCE
- · ATTACHMENT AND DETACHMENT
- · DOUBT AND CERTAINTY
- · DISCORD AND PEACE

4. Frithjof Schuon, *The Play of Masks* (Bloomington, IN: World Wisdom Books, 1992), p. 1.

We have chosen to highlight certain sentiments in view of their counterpart in the netherworld of failed aspiration and unfulfilled emotion—the hunger, despair, fear, attachment, doubt, and turmoil that is the lot of the average person—in order to more fully appreciate the significance and richness of the higher emotions available in the field of human perception. In addition, each of these sentiments begins in the inadequacy of their counterpart and the emotive frustration experienced as a result of the life of this world. Thus, certainty begins in doubt, reverence finds its complement in fear, and hope evolves out of despair. Our belief system implies consequences and requires a suitable response to the demands brought about by what we choose to believe. In this way, people can formulate valid replies to their initial intuition of God and the overpowering attraction they feel for the Supreme Being, through an intimacy that awakens a full range of sacred emotions and sensibilities within the heart.

HUNGER AND DESIRE

The intuition of God represents initially a knowledge rather than a feeling, and is born of a spiritual instinct that originates within the faculty of the human intellect as an awakening that comes to reside in the mind and heart as an operative knowledge in confronting the reality of this world. Thus, we begin our exposé of the emotions with human desire and envision the act of yearning as born of a fundamental hunger of mind, heart, and soul that needs to be filled with any number of sentiments and emotions, but that will be filled with nothing without the active pursuit of seeking, of yearning, and of searching beyond the confines of the individual self in order to reconnect with the Sacred Origin and Absolute Center that is the natural and indeed the only true object of our veneration and that indeed lies sequestered within us as the kernel of our own truth.

Hunger, and the gnawing privation that hunger symbolizes, is not just the insatiable craving for food and material objects that modern society has come to emulate as the sole *raison d'être* of its desire. Hunger is an aboriginal condition that is native to human existence. It seizes the body with a perennial craving that demands to be satisfied and invades our conscious experience at every turn with its defining sense of deprivation and loss. It affects not only the body with its call to satisfaction and fulfillment; it also involves the mind, the psyche, the heart, and the soul with its sense of contingency and its feelings of ungratified desire. It demands to be addressed and will not go unnoticed.

This desire of human beings, embodied on its lowest level in a hunger for that which they have not, is prefigured on a higher level in their instinctive yearning and desire for God. There is something within human beings that will lead them to the perfection of their being and the transcendence of their soul, and this something finds its origin and point of departure in hunger. At its most elemental level of experience this begins within the stomach, but eventually seeps into the very pores of the being on intellectual, emotional, and psychological levels to manifest as a fundamental desire to transcend the conditions of this world and the limitations of the body for that otherworldly, primordial experience that still lies deep within as a remembrance of the perfection and happiness that is implicit in the satisfaction of humanity's symbolic, primal hunger. As such, this kind of raw, transcending hunger is the mode of experience most desired and favored by true seekers after the truth, far beyond the limiting satisfaction that any physical satiety could possibly bring.

DESPAIR AND HOPE

If hope means the sweet anticipation of the soul for salvation in the celestial Paradise, then despair is a mental adaptation and psychic prelude of the soul for a lasting damnation. Despair is the darkest of all emotions, and is even considered by some to be sufficient ground for the termination of life and the edge beyond which lies the descent into the sheer misery of an enduring hopelessness. As an emotion with a broad range of influence, despair is not just the notation of the end of meaning and the suspension of desire for all future possibility, it is the beginning of an impending doom that awaits but never arrives, that buds but never blooms, that promises but never fulfills. It raises its malevolent head and makes itself known when all else fails—most notably when the mind, heart, psyche, and soul of a person denies everything and affirms nothing with respect to the life of the spirit. When the particular destiny of a given life entity no longer has any frame of reference beyond the contingencies of this world or a meaningless death, then despair moves into the void and seizes the mind and heart of a person with a vengeance beyond reckoning.

Only one antidote exists to the world of hopelessness and despair and that is the assurance of hope implicit in faith. Hope is the natural antipode of despair and the only reasonable solution to the bitterness of its hopelessness. Everything about the life of the spirit awakens feelings of hope within human beings, from the knowledge of a unified, enduring, and eternal reality as an alternative to the fleeting, transient, and contingent reality we experience in this world, to the promise of a return to the perfection and grace that is prefigured in the primordial paradise and that we instinctively feel within us as an inward reality. Deliverance is the ultimate desire of the human mentality; it is the fulfillment of our hope to be free of the constraints of the earthly mold and the limitations of the purely human framework. "God will deliver the righteous to their place of salvation: No evil shall touch them, nor shall they grieve" (Quran 39:61).

The symbol of salvation is none other than the garden the faithful have been promised according to the Quran, "Therein will be thrones raised on high, goblets placed (ready), and cushions set in rows" (Quran 88:13-15), a garden that recalls the Golden Age when primordial Adamic man walked with God, talked with God, and as such experienced the knowledge of God directly. Thus, it is a primordial memory as well as a primal, instinctive hope within us that yearns for that which we once enjoyed in principle, but irrevocably lost as an earthly privilege. Hope is a sacred motif that is woven within our very fabric. Our earthly hope resides in the knowledge of God and the voice of universal hope will lead us down the straight path, which in Islam is none other than the path of ascension "of those who receive Your blessings, nor of those who receive Your anger, nor of the damned" (Quran 1:7).

FEAR AND REVERENCE

Fear has two faces. Initially, fear is understood to come to life and grow out of the confrontation with the unknown in life. It seizes the mind and heart of humanity with the tenacious grip of its fearful unknowing and refuses to let us pass through the world without the latent apprehension and anxiety that is the bedrock of the life of this world. The world of the spirit translates the psychotic fear of the unknown into a reverential fear of the Supreme Being, a fear akin to veneration and awe that ultimately expresses itself as worship of the Lord our God. According to Fakhr ad-Din ar-Razi, one of the great commentators on the Quran: "The worship of the heart is fear and hope and the worship of the spirit is surrender and satisfaction in God."[5] The other face of fear is perhaps best summarized by the biblical saying of Solomon: "The fear of the Lord is the beginning of wisdom" (Proverbs 1:7; 9:10). In this sense, fear becomes an act of worship, which represents a true knowledge that prefigures an internalized wisdom. The Sufi mystic Ansari was able to capture the dual nature of fear with the following insight of the true object of a person's fear: "Others fear what the morrow may bring. I am afraid of what happened yesterday."[6] Modern humanity fears the uncertainty of an unknown future; traditional humanity feared the consequences of its actions set within a context of its own past.

If fear is born in the mystery of the unknown, then reverence and awe come to fulfilment in the knowledge of the reality of the Supreme Being. The sentiments of fear and reverence complement each other within the heart of the individual and create a balance between the terror of the unknown mystery and the compelling awe of that which is worshiped as the unknown revelation. Fear brings us face to face with the Divine Mystery, while reverence responds to that mystery with feelings of awe and veneration in the light of the divine disclosures of revelation. In every encounter with the Divinity, as in the recitation of the Quran, or partaking of the sacrament of Communion, there must be an element of fear in which the unknown mystery will never be fully revealed or resolved, and there must be an accompanying reverential awe when the human entity is permitted to experience through higher emotion and sacred sentiment the inner reality of the Divine Secret, however brief may be the moment of true encounter. The beginning of the second chapter of the Quran, the *Sura al-Baqara*, immediately identifies those for whom the revealed Book is intended: "this is the Book; in it is certain guidance, without any doubt, for those who fear God" (2:2).

5. Quoted in Charles Le Gai Eaton, *Islam and the Destiny of Man* (Albany, NY: SUNY Press, 1985), p. 61.
6. Ansari, quoted in Eknath Easwaran (ed.), *God Makes the Rivers to Flow: Sacred Literature of the World* (Tomales, CA: Nilgiri Press, 2003), p. 134.

ATTACHMENT AND DETACHMENT

In today's modern-day environment, the heart is no longer the field of encounter between the Divine and the human; the soul is no longer connected with the abiding Spirit that created it. Modern human beings are now attached to the world. Their attachment to God has been replaced by the world of forms, the world of possessions, and the illusion of progress toward some ill-defined future plenitude in this life. The plane of encounter is between the individual ego and the world. In the process, human beings have become a mirror reflection of themselves, anticipating the part of pure selfishness, rather than the reflection of the greater Self envisioned by the various traditions. They are no longer an open book awaiting the words of the Divine Pen to inscribe Its destiny on their soul; they deny the meeting with their Creator and therefore deny the promise of their own future on other levels of reality.

Still, the human being has yet to fully realize the paradox that lies at the heart of earthly existence. If a person loves the world, they become attached to its tempting artifacts and lose the instinctive attachment to the Divinity. Yet, feelings of attachment to God require separation from the attractions of the world. Spiritual progress moves from separation, through attachment, to a pure and free detachment of mind and heart from the turmoil and pressures of life. Separation from the world automatically attaches a person to God. This leads not to a denial of the world as such, but to a refined detachment of soul from the external forces and pressures that are inevitable on the dissonant plane of earth, a detachment that is fueled by the serenity and calm repose offered by the certitudes of spiritual knowledge and a living, practical wisdom. Within the mode of separation, everything matters less and less with regard to the world; within the mode of attachment, everything matters more and more with regard to God; within the mode of detachment, nothing at all matters, except God.

The virtue of detachment, however, dignifies and brings to fulfillment what separation and attachment can only commence and approximate. Detachment is nothing short of the realization that any true separation from God is futile, if not impossible. It exudes a sublime disinterest to the allurements and attractions of the world. Indeed, detachment could be called the virtue of virtues, since it renders the world's offerings as valueless illusions in which only an insecure and naive ego could possibly take part. Moreover, if all that detachment accomplished for the soul was an indifference to the world, it would already prove its own precious value; but detachment also addresses itself to life's turmoil and uncertainty. It represents an inner calm as a response to all that rudely confronts people during the course of their lives. It proposes an active repose of the soul that renders our aspiration to God as meaningful and our addiction to the world as meaningless. Moreover, the feeling of detachment brings to the human consciousness a surprisingly subtle insight: If a person is truly saved by the compassion, mercy, and love of God, what need is there for the world, for the ego, or for the individual self. These lesser gods are all rendered superfluous in the face of the divine alternative, and "God is sufficient" (Quran 3:173).

DOUBT AND CERTAINTY

It is a *conditio sine qua non* of human existence that, without the aid of a first principle, human beings suffer from feelings of perennial doubt concerning the fundamental questions of origin, meaning, and ultimate end that shape their world. It is true that humanity has the faculty of reason with which to navigate its way through the dilemmas and contingencies of life, and this reason has proven to be rational, logical, and balanced, so far as it goes. However, far from being the receptacle of a higher knowledge and the filter of an intuitive perception that arrives directly from above, human reason is a *tabula rasa* that merely processes the thoughts and impressions the mind sets forth. What, after all, are the facts that modern scientists assemble but the observations of the senses and physical matter, which are then submitted to human reason to sort out and integrate into a meaningful and integrated whole. Superficially, the facts established by modern science are indeed convincing and their coherent physicality, their formal beauty, and their practical utility are a wonder to behold; but what is the source of this scientific knowledge? What gives the bodily senses the right to establish the criterion of reality, and what are the grounds for objectivity that things actually are in truth what the senses represent them to be? If anything, the answer to this question—if one exists in the mind of an individual at all—is cast in the shadow of a recurring and persistent human doubt concerning the fundamental mysteries, whose understanding perennially eludes our grasp.

Because the divine mystery refuses to give up the mystique of its elemental secrets, a feeling of certainty continues to elude modern humanity. It is becoming increasingly clear that it is not the quantity of accumulated scientific knowledge but rather the quality of a realized wisdom that will create a feeling of inner certainty that people can rely on. Ultimately, the only thing that truly matters to humankind is whether the knowledge of the absolute Reality is true and whether it lives in the mind as an enduring certainty. The vision of a metaphysical knowledge, of eternal and supernatural realities, is rooted in first principles that are conveyed through revelation, through nature, and through humankind. It is a principial knowledge that begins with revelation, becomes internalized through the intuition of that knowledge and the premonition of faith, and ends with feelings of certainty that are definitive and absolute.

The modern mentality demands certainty of proof without realizing that certainty is more precisely a feeling rather than a knowledge. Believers can witness the unfolding of their external destiny in the light of the sacred truths that give shape, definition, and color to their experience here on earth. Their life is not shaded with doubt or despair in the face of the unknown forces of nature. The believers' faith challenges the fundamental mystery of existence with the certainty of a revealed knowledge. Doubt only surrenders a person to unknown forces as they seek a knowledge that can lend meaning to the vicissitudes and uncertainties in life. The ultimate evidence and the final proof can never be the object of humanity's search, either on the physical, mental, or the spiritual plane, because no such evidence exists, while the answer to life's mystery lies far beyond any arbitrary proof. Are we objective beings, armed with the tools of mind and matter, in search of a subject, as modern science would have us believe; or are we subjective beings, armed with intelligence and free will in search of the Objective, the relative in search of the Absolute, the human fragment in search of the Whole?

There exists a precarious balance between doubt and certainty within the human condition that requires the effort of spiritual disciplines in order to be maintained. On the one hand, truth is enigmatic enough to keep some people guessing about life's fundamental truths to the point that they are unable to recognize or withstand truth's reality; on the other hand, only the truth of the one Reality still has the power to overwhelm us with its sublimity, its simplicity, and its certainty, negating not only all falsehood and ignorance, but also all that is profane, relative, and illusory in the world. In doubt, we are adrift in a negative sentimentality that keeps us wandering on the periphery of existence; in certainty, we are enveloped within a sacred sentiment that places us within the Absolute Center and the Primordial Point. "Certainty, being an aspect of knowledge, is situated beyond the domain of the sentiments but on the individual plane it nonetheless possesses a perfume which allows us to look on it as a sentiment."[7]

DISCORD AND PEACE

The feelings of disharmony and discord that characterize the modern world are the inward expression of an outward imbalance that exists between the inner person and the external world. People today demand proofs of an inner, universal reality from an existential creation that has no power to objectify the true nature of reality but that is merely the causal manifestation of the true reality. The human condition cannot be defined by the physical parameters of the external world; to want to reduce the mystery and the miracle of the human being as a microcosm in reflection of the great macrocosm is to place oneself at the disposition of the vicissitudes and contingencies of that world and nothing more. The result is the experience of a world full of discord and a world in turmoil, revealing a level of disharmony and imbalance that is frightening to behold, but not the kind of reverential fear that we expressed with reference to the sublime concept of a Supreme Deity.

As an unassailable alternative, modern humanity still has revelation as the ultimate source of knowledge, a knowledge whose certainty cannot be questioned and whose truth is eternal. Within the Islamic tradition, for instance, the Quran as revelation addresses the broad expanse of all human endeavor, enlightens humanity on all the mysteries of the human condition, and places the human entity within a universal context that is fully integrating and deeply satisfying. The profound doctrinal themes, the great ethical questions, and the ennobling sacred sentiments all reflect the fundamental elements that constitute the human condition and provide

7. Frithjof Schuon, *Logic and Transcendence*, p. 163.

a framework of spirituality that takes account of the knowledge (doctrine), the behavior (ethical morality), and the higher sentiment (virtue) of humankind within the earthly setting.

The disharmony and turmoil of life are counterbalanced by the serenity and peace that is the promise of a conscious surrender (*islam*) to God. The uncertainty reflected in the perennial mystery of life is counterbalanced by the absolute quality and the certainty that is the lodestone of the word of God. The imbalance and disequilibrium of the human soul is counterbalanced by the stability and equilibrium implicit in the knowledge of the one Reality. The forgetfulness of our self-identity is counterbalanced by the consciousness of the greater Self. The density of the earthly and the mundane is offset by the ethereal quality of the mystic and the spiritual. The linear quality of the strictly horizontal perception is transfigured by the alchemical quality of the vertical disclosure. Finally, the endless diversity and multiplicity of this world is counterbalanced—indeed resolved—by the unity and oneness of the Transcendent Center.

The rational psyche of modern times wishes to preserve the lower, individual self on some primitive instinctive level, but in surrendering to the greater Self, it will receive in return the one thing it wishes to gain on some primordial instinctive level, namely the peace of mind and tranquility of heart that is the holy sentiment of the submissive soul, resulting in the final effacement of the individual in which the shadow self of the ego is completely enveloped in the radiant light of the Universal Self.

Chapter Six

♣

The Sacred Ground of the Soul

Was somebody asking to see the soul? See your own shape and countenance, persons, substances, beasts, the trees, the running rivers, the rocks and sands.
(Walt Whitman)

Then shall the dust return to the earth as it was; and the spirit shall return unto God who gave it.
(Ecclesiastes 12:7)

The Quran warns the faithful not to ask intrusive questions about the hidden nature of the Spirit. An acclaimed verse reveals: "Say: the Spirit is at the Command of my Lord" (17:85). This injunction, however, does not preclude our asking questions about the human soul: What is it? Where is it? What does it mean? Where will it lead us? These are only some of the perennial questions whose answer would certainly shape the way a person understands their place in the universe and may even change the course of their individual destiny. Let us proceed with this delicate inquiry and see where it leads us.

Searching for the soul of a person is like searching for the soul of the forest or the soul of the mountain. you know it lies within the natural order of Nature as a living presence but you cannot put your finger on it. The soul presence lies in every created thing as a unique outpouring of an individual and distinctive essence, as though the spirit of a thing has disappeared into the physical object of a body, a tree, or a drop of water—only to leave behind its mystery and numinous glow as a soulprint in tribute to its existence. It is as if the true identity is concealed in such small matters as a blade of grass or the shadow of a man or woman, making the natural world of plants, animals, and humankind as advertisements for the sublime world of the spirit, however little we are able to understand their secret messages.

We repeat here a truth alien to the modern mentality but second nature to the more traditional one: namely, that the soul constitutes the sacred ground of our being. As a truth, it is inviolate, identifying the essence of our inner being as grounded within a soul that is a direct reflection of the Spirit of God, who, according to the Quranic revelation (32:9), blew His Spirit into the corporeal form of humankind, thereby making us now and forever an immortal being cast into the shape of a mortal person. As an idea, it is as simple as it is profound, reaching deep into the inner depths in order to substantiate and articulate what lies at the root of the being, and which radiates outward into every cell of the body as the animating quality of life. Without soul, there is no such thing as a created form, much less the living presence of a human person.

Why, then, is the concept of the soul so difficult for the modern mind to accept, while instead its sublime presence within the human body as its chief animating quality is forgotten? Is it merely because modern science has not been able to reduce the human soul to the subatomic particles of the quantum world and has no intention of doing so? Is it because the soul does not fit, and will never fit, into the parametric principles of the empirical inquiry? Alternatively, is there a darker side to modern humanity's denial of the inward reality, a side so determined and malefic that it has the potential power to destroy the very soul and spirit that makes us what we are according to the traditional point of view, a living revelation and a human symbol of the highest truth?

Curiously enough, no modern argument even exists about the true nature of the soul; it has simply disappeared as a serious consideration from the rational horizon of mind predominant within the scientific community of scholars. Human intelligence is not doubted by modern science; but its origin, focus, manner of operation, and ultimate goal is perceived to be matter-based and therefore quite different from the traditional notion of intelligence, perennially considered to have a luminous source as its first origin and the knowledge of God as its final end. Similarly, we have already reflected upon the differences in understanding concerning the other faculties and fields of perception. Our reason, heart, sacred emotions and sentiments, our aboriginal, primordial instincts, and our spiritual imagination are all understood within a certain modern-day context that takes its inspiration, not from the traditional sources of knowledge prescribed by the religions and inscribed within our heart, but rather from the contemporary worldview of modern science and its on-going research into the empirical nature of the human faculties.

Unlike the mind and the other higher faculties, there is no split perception concerning the soul's significance and meaning. Modern science has so much trouble with the traditional concept of the soul that it dismisses its existence outright as a mystery with no name, a myth and possibly even an anachronism, or else the shadowy phantom of an archaic system of thought that is not worth rational consideration. It does not even entertain the idea of the soul and makes no attempt to associate its existence with any physical property within us, as it does with the mind, human intelligence, and self-consciousness,[1] all elements of humanity that remain mysterious but that are well on the way to being reduced by scientists to the purely physical properties found within nature and governed by natural laws. The soul, however, refuses to give up its holy ghost and undergo the empirical test of scientific scrutiny; its presence lies veiled within us as the invisible backcloth of our being where it eludes scientific inquiry. As a consequence, the soul is no longer a serious contender within the modern mentality as the locus of our individuality and the living truth of our vital being.

How then are we to approach the soul, witness the power of its hidden presence, understand its dynamic force, and make it a part of our consciousness as a living reality within our lives? Perhaps the best answer, given the contingencies of the modern world, would be to approach the subject in fear and trepidation lest a profound desire to be modern leaves us beyond the parameter of the circle of truth. Instead, we turn to the world of tradition where the traditional language and the essential knowledge of God can be found in revealed scripture and the spiritual doctrines contained within the perennial philosophy of the major religions. In our inquiry into the soul, what we first encounter is none other than the sacred symbols of the earth, the "breath" and the "wind" of God, in order to

---

1. Nothing is considered so sacred anymore that it could claim to be beyond the reach of the reductionists who want to reduce every intangible quality and inner aspect of the human entity to a purely biological, molecular, or subatomic manifestation. In addition to mind and consciousness, the reduction of human emotion, human nature, and even the manifestation of culture to purely physical properties are now considered serious objects of scientific study. "The main thrust of the consilience world view . . . is that culture and hence the unique qualities of the human species will make complete sense only when linked in causal explanation to the natural sciences. Biology in particular is the most proximate and hence relevant of the scientific disciplines" (E. O. Wilson, *Consilience*, p. 292).

compress within these traditional sacred symbols the inexpressible and indeed invisible image of the soul within every man, woman, and child.

According to the Biblical account, all animals received a life-giving spirit, a *nefesh* in Hebrew, or animal soul; however within the human being, according to the Talmud, the Creator placed a soul, referred to in Hebrew as the *neshamah*. The *neshamah* is therefore what ultimately distinguishes the human kingdom from the animal kingdom. "And the Lord formed man (*adam*)[2] from the dust of the ground (*adamah*) and blew into his nostrils a soul of life (*neshamah*), and the man became a living being (*nefesh*)" (Genesis 2:7). Interestingly enough, the Hebrew word *adam* has its root in the Hebrew word *adamah*, meaning soil, making the human body an earth creation that gives Adam his name.

The English word "soul" comes from the German word *Seele*, the Gothic *saiwala*, and the old German *saiwalo*, which is connected to the Greek *aioli*, meaning mobile, colored, and iridescent. The word "spirit" is generally associated with the Latin word *animus* (spirit) and *anima* (soul), the luminous and pneumatic principle, sometimes referred to as the gate of the Spirit which "bloweth where it listeth" (John 3:8). In Old High German, *spiritus Sanctus* was rendered as *attune*, breath. The Greek *animus* meaning wind recalls another Greek word for wind, *pneumatic*, which also refers to spirit. The Hindu tradition refers to *atman* which assumes a derivation from the root *an* or *van* meaning to breathe or blow. These unique affinities show that through a variety of languages, including Latin, Greek, German, and even Sanskrit, the names given to the soul are related to the concept of wind, "moving air," and "the cold breath of the spirit."

In Arabic, the Quranic terms for spirit and soul also have connotations of air: *ruh* refers to spirit and *rih* means wind, while *nafs* and *nafas* have the same root and refer to the breath. Echoing the

2. The traditional Jewish writer Maimonides included an astounding comment in his *The Guide for the Perplexed*, when he suggested that certain animals coexisted with Adam at the time of the creation, who appeared human in shape and also had a form of intelligence, but lacked the "image" which distinguishes humanity from the other animals, Adam having been made in the image of God. The reference to "other animals" refers to the primates and hominids of pre-historic time who are now considered to be the uncles and cousins of humanity, while the "image" is none other than the Spirit of God.

perennial unity of concepts within the various religions, the Quran emphasizes the concept that the breath is derived from the Spirit of God since He "breathed into him [Adam] of My Spirit" (15:29).[3] According to Islamic doctrine, it is through the soul (*nafs*) that the devil (*shaytan*) can obtain a hold on the human being, whereas the spirit (*ruh*) whose essence is pure light lies beyond the reach of the devil. The qualitative uniqueness of humanity and our living quality derives from the Spirit of God, otherwise we would be a body without a soul, which according to the various traditions makes no sense at all. When the spirit is present within the body, it manifests as a soul that is prone to all the contingencies of this world.

We mention a body without a soul, echoing the sentiment of the modern scientific community; and yet the concept sounds curiously hollow, shocking even, and ultimately false because it belies the self-image of the human person. What would we have been, what would we be, and what would we become without the soul essence as the absolute ground of our being? In today's view, we know from biology and its related sciences that the body is composed of cells, genetic material, proteins, DNA and the like; chemistry speaks of molecules and chemical composites, while physicists refer to protons, neurons, and other rarefied elements in the quantum world of subatomic particles. Do these constituent elements add up to a human being? The scientific community would like us to believe that they do.

Due to the modern-day campaign to come to philosophic terms with a purely empirical humankind, volumes have been written to identify the constituent parts of the physical person, who is inevitably reduced to a form of proto-matter in the guise of a highly evolved body whose living quality, while still a mystery without a clear origin, is defined in terms of probabilities that might never have occurred if we were not here to substantiate our existence. Without a soul, we would become merely a thing, an inert mass, and no longer the free spirit and sublime reflection of the qualities and attributes of God; without a soul, we would be visibly outward and spiritually neutral, without any enduring consequence, a mere fact rather than a living

---

3. Hence the importance of the breath as the symbolic image of the soul. The Quran (3:44) confirms that the breath also serves as the vehicle of the soul when it says that the breath of Jesus could quicken the dead.

truth. As a result, modern science and the worldview that it engenders must live with the consequences of the philosophy it espouses through its empirical findings.

People, even scientists, living in more traditional societies sought to understand the nature and workings of the natural order, but they never claimed matter as the sole reality that had no counterpart in an unseen world. Matter was not something separated from spirit but was rather its necessary complement and a creation and function of God. Today, the very word "soul" in its traditional meaning has been all but eliminated from the vocabulary of modern thinking.[4] Throughout recorded history, however, the thread of spiritual inquiry within the religious traditions, together with the accompanying philosophical speculation, was always concerned with the true nature of our essential live-giving identity, namely the soul.

Plato says, "There is something in the soul that bids men drink and something that forbids" (*Republic* 439). In referring to the soul, he draws on different concepts in order to come to terms with a reality difficult to comprehend. He speaks of the "Leader" within us by many names, including Reason, Mind, Genius, and most Divine, the best of ourselves being the ruling and the eternal part, the Immortal Soul that "is our real Self" (*Laws* 959A). It is referred to by Philo as "soul of the soul," by Hermes as "Good Genius." It has been called the self of the Self, the Immortal Leader, and the Inner Controller in the Vedic tradition which makes the statement that it is this (Holy) "Ghost" that we give up when we die which leads to the question: "In whom, when I go forth, shall I be going forth?" (Prashna Upanishad 6.3)[5]

The idea of the soul defies clear mathematical definition and cannot be described in the empirical language of modern science. As the subject in its own inquiry, modern humanity loses sight of our origins in the vast beginnings of time when the human soul simply disappears into the antediluvian forest with the traces of early

4. One has only to think of the expressions such as "soul music" or "soul food" to realize just how far the modern mentality has strayed from the traditional meaning of the word "soul," while still drawing on a dim residue of meaning to convey a sentimental feeling of the heart generated by these expressions.
5. Cf. Ananda Coomaraswamy, *What is Civilization? And Other Essays* (Great Barrington, MA: Lindisfarne Press, 1989), p. 36.

humanity's footsteps. The inner landscape of the soul has been laid bare and the recollections of sanctity and the forces of the spirit that once nourished the soul have been set behind a veil that may never be lifted. Yet, the human soul continues to lay claim to us, and its presence in the form of the human spirit continues to be felt by people in their experiences of everyday life. We have had no part in its coming and we cannot account for its existence; but exist it does, for there is a light within us that no other animal has ever had, a light and a presence that refuses to disappear, in spite of the fact that modern science cannot account for it and will never classify it on its own terms.

♣ ♣ ♣

Modern humanity searches through the debris of subatomic particles for what traditional believers had already found in revelation, namely knowledge of origins, of identity, of meaning, and of our ultimate purpose and final end. Biologists dig deep into the constituent parts of our being in search of the living source of our existence; they have developed a grand architecture of life that traces itself back to a single cellular source, but the spontaneous swamp-like interface that should have occurred miraculously between earth and water at the place of the origin of protozoan life cannot be proved and must remain as a theory that has never come to pass.

In spite of what some scientists refer to as the inherent "improbability of life,"[6] life's mysterious appearance occurred almost immediately on the newly formed planet Earth and even in its simple form contained the complex genetic material that we now call DNA and RNA. The idea that, given enough geologic time, anything is possible,[7] even the spontaneous eruption of life, is belied by the fact that single-celled organisms existed on the earth since the time of its early formation and not after a sufficient geologic time had

6. James Lovelock, *The Ages of Gaia: A Biography of Our Living Earth* (New York: Bantam Books, 1990), p. 25.
7. "Time is in fact the hero of the plot [in the generation of the first form of life]. . . . Given so much time, the 'impossible' becomes the possible, the possible probable, and the probable virtually certain. One has only to wait: time itself performs the miracles" (George Wald, "The Origin of Life," *Scientific American* 191 (August 1954), p. 48).

elapsed to allow a pre-biotic evolution to take place among the innumerable combinations of chemical elements. The search thus goes on for an explanation of the origin of the life force, which can set forth a description that meets the strict requirements of the rational and scientific community.[8]

In the world of fossils, paleontologists search, not for the soul of humanity, for that would echo too much of the traditional attitude they so forcefully want to deny; instead, they search for what they euphoniously call our humanity. The well-known paleontologist Richard Leakey writes reflectively:

> Because the target of the search is we ourselves, the enterprise takes on a dimension absent from other sciences. It is in a sense extra-scientific, more philosophical and metaphysical, and it addresses questions that arise from our need to understand the nature of humanity and our place in the world.[9]

Paleontologists see themselves as the harbingers of a philosophy of humanity that will ensue through their findings in the incredible world of fossils, although a profound ambivalence shines through much of their writings, which betray a fundamental insecurity with regards to their mandate. Leakey takes the materialist—and reductionist—view that consciousness, as one of the key defining factors of our humanity, is "the product of the brain's activity, not some gossamer attachment to the organ."[10] If in the world of fossils we seek our soul, we are forced to draw it from the empty sockets of skulls or the representations of artists who might project their own conceptions of the past upon these beings who are long since dead and cannot defend themselves against the exotic speculations of modern scientists.

Modern psychology, on the other hand, makes distinctions of kind and quality with regard to the human psyche. Psychologists are in search of what they define as the modern psyche and its link with the collective unconscious, but even the psyche falls prey to the

8. See my earlier work *Modern Man at the Crossroads: The Encounter of Modern Science and Traditional Knowledge* (Chicago: Kazi Publications, 1999) for an in-depth analysis of modern and traditional thinking on the elusive subject of origins.
9. Richard Leakey and Roger Lewin, *Origins Reconsidered: In Search of What Makes Us Human* (New York: Doubleday, 1992), p. xvi.
10. *Ibid.*, p. 280.

reductionist theories that shape the mentality of our time. According to one of the fathers of modern psychology, C. G. Jung,

> Today the psyche does not build itself a body, but on the contrary, matter, by chemical action, produces the psyche. This reversal of outlook would appear ludicrous if it were not one of the outstanding features of the spirit of the age.[11]

If mind is considered an epiphenomenon of matter, the same conclusion must be reached about the psyche, if not the brain, the hormones, and the instinctual drives. The spirit of the age dictates the attitude that the human psyche is primarily a reflection of everything we call corporeal, empirical, and mundane, while consciousness is understood to be the *conditio sine qua non* of the psychic life. The life of the psyche is understood to be the summary of all that is subjective within the human being as a "gossamer attachment" to the mind; perhaps this is why the term psychological has taken on the flavor of the purely subjective as opposed to the objective reality associated with the human soul, which was the attitude of the traditional people of former times.

In contrast to the prevailing spirit of the modern era, which finds its sustenance in the philosophic conclusions drawn from the discoveries of the biologists, chemists, and paleontologists of our time, the traditional spirit portrays the human soul otherwise. It has, over the millennia, insisted upon the importance of the soul as the life force and animating principle of humanity's essential being. If the soul exists, it is not as the result of the accumulation of material residues released into the atmosphere of the body as psychic coagulations and psychological knots; but rather, it exists as the quintessence of the human being, and draws its source from a spiritual principle in order to become the life force of the body and its living truth. In this view, human beings are composed of layers, the corporeal layer being the most restricted modality of their individual human manifestation and the lowest order in the hierarchy of manifestation. Needless to say, a person cannot believe this and call himself modern, since to be modern is to deny such a possibility; but not everyone lives to be modern and some people still wish to

[11] Carl Jung, *Modern Man in Search of a Soul*, trans. W. Dell and Cary Baynes (New York: Harcourt Brace Jovanovich, 1933), pp. 175-176.

live in a world that does not sacrifice its implicit truth for the sake of an expedient curiosity.

The more traditional mentality believed in the concept of the soul as the ultimate locus of human individuality; the soul was the ground upon which the personal being invested in a principle not rooted exclusively in themselves. Behind the intuition of higher truth, behind all the emotive experience that colors and shapes our inner world, behind all the sacred sentiments and virtues that can result from the rich texture of a human life, behind the free will and the wisdom that adds to the qualitative uniqueness of the human being, behind all the seeing and hearing of our senses, and deeper than the deepest thought lies the human soul as the source of the individual being. As source and sentinel outpost of the inner faculties, the soul provides the mind, the consciousness, the heart, the emotions, and the imagination with the "presence"—for want of a better word—that these faculties need to fulfill their mandate within the borderland of the spirit. The entire hue and ambiance of the soul grows and develops in accordance with the relationship it establishes between the two sides of its own reality, the world of the spirit and the world of the body.

We do not necessarily know the soul as knowledge and we may not be able to locate or prove it in a way acceptable to the modern scientific mentality, but we sense it as an experience, indeed it is *the* defining experience of our being. People know that they are not the body because the body is not the source of their identity. It plays its part as a vehicle of movement and as an instrument of the inner faculties,[12] but it is not the summary of who they are; on the contrary it is merely the visual and corporeal image of a deeper self. People know that they are not the mind because the mind is an ever-changing and fickle ideogram that records the impressions of outer and inner worlds but which is also subject to the instability and turmoil of the emotions. People know through experience that there is something within their being and on which they cannot put their finger, and that has no pulse like the beating of the heart, and yet it serves as a witness for all that we are and do, an observer that needs to be recognized "as such" and "as is."

12. Hindu tradition refers to the body as the chariot of the mind.

There comes a moment when we can only speak of the soul through symbols and metaphors because its subtle form makes it difficult to come to terms with its chief defining quality. We think of the soul as if it were a cup that we fill with all the light and darkness of each moment throughout the course of our life. We think of the soul in terms of the ground of our being in which the action of a lifetime takes root and as the field in which our desires are played out. We think of the soul as a pivot, reflecting the good and evil, the light and darkness that represent the polarity of the world. We speak of the soul as a bridge between the world of the body and the world of the spirit, a mediatory function in the same way that the human being serves as a mediator between Heaven and Earth.

The soul is the witness identified but never witnessed and the source searched for but never found. As witness and source, it observes but is never observed, and creates the framework of our being without becoming an identifiable point of reference. It is everywhere and nowhere, as with its symbolic counterpart the breath, invisible in itself, but ubiquitous and vivifying like the air, and perceptible through an incredible range of dynamic functions. As the inmost self, it represents the kernel of the husk or as Frithjof Schuon expresses it, the "naturally supernatural kernel of the individual."[13]

As the very ground of our being, it provides the interior soil in which the outward personality can take root in order to become the field of impressions and experiences within a given life. It makes what we experience uniquely ours and not someone else's. We sense the existence of the soul in the same way that we sense the consciousness that we are ourselves and not another person. While human consciousness may provide the ambiance for self-awareness and set the tone for reflection, the soul provides the framework and field with which to absorb all the outer and inner experiences of our lives into the accumulation of what becomes the unified continuum of an individual human spirit.

How do we sense the soul? Who can say for sure; for everyone has their own experience of the inner self. The consciousness of existence and the reality of being oneself is a unique and precious

13. Frithjof Schuon, *Light on the Ancient Worlds* (London: Perennial Books, 1965), p. 136.

truth. We sense it in the integrity and durability of our individuality, which remains true to itself throughout the course of a life, for in some strange way, we are the same person passing through different phases of a life experience, an evolving ego that changes and yet is housed within the same continuum of presence that is the individual soul.

We experience the finite quality of the ego and the world through wealth, fame, friends, work, and personal achievement, indeed through our very own bodies; but we sense the Infinite and actually experience it by virtue of the existence of the soul. Finally, we sense the soul through the force of our free will. If we ask ourselves what is the essential element of our being, there is no better indicator as to who we are than through the metronome of our desires and their inevitable consequences. What we present to the world are but fragments of ourselves in the form of a personable ego that meets the world head on; but the underlying essence that supports the complete being remains within as the true "I" of the abiding self and the venue and ground in which the inner battle for the perfection of the individual takes place.

♣　♣　♣

The soul is not a final destination or an end in itself; it serves a mediatory function as bridge between worlds. As such, it forms the final piece in the puzzle we have created in this work in order to portray the rarefied experience of the higher faculties within the borderland of the spirit. The human soul takes its own journey according to its inborn nature, subject to the contingencies of the era in which it lives. Plotinus has made reference to the soul's journey: "It shall come, not to another, but to itself."[14] The journey of the soul moves from the outer world of the natural environment and the experience of the body, to the inner world of the mind, heart, imagination, and spiritual instincts, only to come to rest within the supra-natural environment of the inner life of the spirit, which throughout the course of a life becomes individualized as the soul of a person. In a strange and curious way, this sacred narrative may sound easy and assured:

14. Plotinus, quoted in Loren Eiseley, *The Unexpected Universe* (New York: Harcourt, Brace, Yovanovich, 1969), p. 24.

the soul summarizes the life and experience of a person and lives on to enter an alternative dimension to this world, namely eternal life; but the experience of the soul is far from easy and never assured.[15] The most important conflicts of a life are fought on the battlefield of the soul, and we have been amply warned by all the great world scriptures that it is possible for us to lose our soul.

Unlike the human intellect, with its direct perception of the knowledge of God and its integral intuition of the numinous realities, the human soul lives in this world in a condition of veiling. The knowledge of God may be available to us through the faculty of our intellect as a direct revelation and as a formal descent of the Spirit of God, but this knowledge is not enough in and of itself and is veiled from our immediate consciousness. Even when this knowledge descends into the mind, it must somehow be internalized within the ground of the soul as a completely absorbed and realized experience.

In fact, the condition of the soul is precarious to say the least. The Sufi sage Mulla Sadra writes: "The soul is the 'junction of the two seas' (Quran 18:59) of corporeal and spiritual things."[16] In other words, the soul stands between the existential condition of the world and the supra-natural condition of the Spirit in the very center of the borderland. As such, it can serve as a medium of light or a medium of darkness. It lies halfway between heaven and earth, between angel and devil, between good and evil. It acts as an intermediary between the luminous, immaterial spirit and the dark, dense matter of the body. "Spirit and body—light and clay—have no common measure. The spirit is one, luminous, subtle, high, and invisible, while the body is many, dark, dense, low, and visible. But the soul is both one and many, luminous and dark, subtle and dense, high and low, invisible and visible."[17]

---

15. Not the least because of the encroaching attitude of modern scientists who are not struck in awe by the sacred story of humanity and have every intention of taking it over as their own: "If the sacred narrative cannot be in the form of a religious cosmology, it will be taken from the material history of the universe and the human species. . . . The true evolutionary epic, retold as poetry, is as intrinsically ennobling as any religious epic. Material reality discovered by science already possesses more content and grandeur than all religious cosmologies combined" (E. O. Wilson, *Consilience*, p. 289).
16. Mulla Sadra, *The Wisdom of the Throne*, trans. J. W. Morris (Princeton, NJ: Princeton University Press, 1981), p. 148.
17. William C. Chittick, *Imaginal Worlds*, p. 71.

The soul does not save the person; the person needs to save their own soul. The body, mind, and heart all take part in the dark drama of earthly life in which the forces of good and evil pull us in opposing directions of light and darkness by cords of fear, desire, forgetfulness and many other conflicting emotions and sentiments. The split personality of the soul is directly affected by a world that is characterized by a fundamental duality, which shapes the coloration and ambiance of life and imprints the very substance of its spirit onto the soul so as to form the personal ground of an individual. We know the dualities of the world for we live the reality of a split existence every day of our lives, including its light and darkness, its good and evil, its truth and falsehood. Would that we could live our lives with a soul that has already resolved its inner conflict by lifting the veil to receive the vision of the Sublime and become one with It. However, the true nature of humanity and the life of this world dictate otherwise.

Direct knowledge of God and a clear unobstructed vision of the Sublime were not meant to be a part of the existential reality of this world. On the contrary, we live a split existence, as if a powerful sword has cut through the center of our being to create the two halves of one self. One side is inherently luminous under the direct influence of the Spirit of God; the other side is characterized by darkness, ignorance, and the habitude of physical and sensate experience. The remembrance of a primordial golden era when the two halves of humanity were one is but a distant memory as well as an aspiration and promise in the soul's journey of return to God. A terrible divide runs down the middle of our beings and through it run all the conceivable manifestations of evil and dispersion that could possibly suit the designs of the devil, who drives the forces of evil through the existential chasm of our being like wild horses through a narrow canyon.

The dual nature of the self is a far more vivid reality within us than the aspiration to be at one with the Divinity. The rift within is deep and dark; it begins as an incomplete and false understanding of the self and its place in the fabric of the world, and ends by overwhelming and dominating the split image of the soul. From deep within this divide emerge the deceit, ignorance, unreality, and illusions of the world; in short, the very face of an existential evil whose false reality boldly challenges the sustaining truth of the Supreme

Good. The true battle[18] of the soul emerges out of this cimmerian gorge of the self, a battle that we must wage every day of our lives if we wish to close the gap that divides the two aspects of the self and confront the existential reality of our lesser selves with the higher reality of the Spirit. As such, the soul is the battleground for this great endeavor.

The Quranic revelation and the Prophetic sayings specifically refer to three distinct dimensions of the soul, which not only characterize its potential condition and state of being, but that also indicate the level of moral and spiritual maturity possible within the individual. It can be mentioned parenthetically that there is an animal soul (*al-nafs al-haywanniyyah*), which is not influenced in any way by the higher faculties and is passively obedient to natural impulses and the incentives of animals within their own domain of experience. The Bible also refers to the life-giving property of the animal soul, which in Hebrew is referred to as the *nefesh* of living beings.

The first of the three distinctively human degrees of soul is called "the soul that commands to evil (*nafs al-ammarah*)" (Quran 12:53). Quite obviously, this is the aspect of the soul that is inclined toward evil, or in modern terms, what we call the passionate and egocentric soul. The second degree of soul is identified as "the soul that blames (*nafs al-lawwamah*)" (Quran 76:2). This is the aspect of the soul that we understand today as conscience, in which the soul blames itself, is aware of its own imperfections and serves as the inner voice that persuades us to repent and turn away from our shortcomings and evils. The third degree of soul is called "the soul at peace (*nafs al-mutma'innah*)" (Quran 89:27). This is an aspect of soul with the potential for perfection and enlightenment resulting in the peace that is the *conditio sine qua non* of the abiding spirit. It is the soul reintegrated into the Spirit and at rest in the certitude of the knowledge of God.

Needless to say, between the petty and self-serving impulses characteristic of the passionate soul (*nafs al-ammarah*) and the integrated and fulfilled achievement of the exalted soul (*nafs al-mutma'innah*) lies the broad expanse of a great, existential battlefield

18. The true battle is the battle to the death, recalling the words of Meister Eckhart: "The soul must put itself to death," and the saying of the Prophet: "Die before you die."

upon which the forces of good and evil, light and darkness, knowledge and ignorance, consciousness and unconsciousness, perfection and imperfection are lived, experienced, and brought to resolution for better or worse. This battle within the inner being recalls a traditional saying of the Prophet when he and his army were returning from the field of battle: "We have returned from the lesser holy war (*al-jihad al-asghar*) to the greater holy war (*al-jihad al-akbar*)." When his companions asked him what exactly he meant by this great battle, he replied: "The struggle against the lower self."

The concept of Islamic *jihad* has received a lot of negative publicity from the media in the recent past, partly through the West's limited understanding of it, and partly from the indiscriminate use of the term by fanatical Islamic militant and fundamentalist groups who have turned it into a slogan for indiscriminate terrorism. The Prophet himself only fought defensive wars in his effort to establish the framework of the nascent religion of Islam and emphasized the importance of the greater *jihad*, or inner struggle, as opposed to the lesser *jihad* of actual physical battle for plunder or territorial gain. The word *jihad* in its Arabic root *j-h-d* means to strive, to make an effort, to exert oneself, emphasizing the Islamic theme of creating equilibrium in all phases of one's individual life so that these efforts might take root within our soul.

The *jihad* is much more than the establishment of a formal religion or the extension of its borders. Contrary to the currently prevailing notion of achieving one's rights or some perceived gain through wholesale terror or aggression, *jihad* strikes at the very heart of our existential challenge to recognize the reality of who we really are and overcome the ignorance and limitation that prevent us from achieving our full potential. The inner *jihad* must be practiced because the soul is veiled from the direct perception of reality. It represents the constant inner war against all that veils us from the Truth and all that destroys our inner equilibrium. Its dual nature is revealed through the expression of the higher and lower soul, or the inmost self that defines and shapes human nature, as opposed to the rational self that now dominates the modern psyche's false identity.

This rational self has become so strong during the present age of empirical science that it has become possible for the superficial, self-oriented ego to ignore, if not completely deny, the existence of the inner self, becoming the most evident symptom of the internal disequilibria within the soul of modern humanity generally.

> To overcome the lethargy, passivity and indifference of the soul, qualities which have become second nature to it as a result of man's forgetting who he really is, constitutes likewise a constant *jihad.* To restrain the soul from dissipating itself outwardly as a result of its centrifugal tendencies and to bring it back to the center, wherein reside Divine Peace and all the beauty which the soul seeks in vain in the domain of multiplicity, this is again an inner *jihad.*[19]

Without the influence of the greater *jihad* within human consciousness—a perennial battle that needs to be fought throughout one's life—the externalizing forces acting upon us and the descent toward darkness and multiplicity cannot be reversed and the purification of the soul cannot be attained. This will then lead us on a downward spiral until we finally arrive at the infrahuman state, in which the anguish of the lost becomes the prelude to damnation.

The choice lies with us to discern the principial knowledge of the truth that we were created to know through an enlightened intelligence, to respond to the natural instinct and the imaginal world of our soul, and to act upon that knowledge through an empowered heart rich in higher emotion and sacred sentiment. The consequences of this endeavor lie within the soul, which bears the imprint of a person's identification of self either as an enlightened being on a sacred journey of return to God, or as a cognitive and thinking animal who has emerged from the dark density of the forest on a journey of evolution toward some uncertain end with no mechanism to resolve the many complexes of the psyche and no way of getting rid of the multiple demons of the lower self.

The true battle of the soul is the principal human mandate. The existential condition of humanity is such that, as the go-between and intermediary between the phenomenal and spiritual worlds, it is charged with the responsibility of strengthening the spiritual light within its being and weakening the bodily darkness. The inner battle is the strengthening of the soul's spiritual dimension through effort, seeking, and striving, not on some theoretical or ethereal

---

19. Seyyed Hossein Nasr, *Traditional Islam in the Modern World* (London: Kegan Paul International, 1987), p. 32.

plane, but rather, on a practical and even rational plane, in which the intelligence, the reason, the mind, the heart, indeed all the faculties of knowing and perception are finely-tuned and focused on the unique truth of the one Reality that leads the soul back towards its reintegration with the Spirit and towards the union of the individual soul with God. Even the breath, as physical symbol for the soul's aspiration and the very principle of life, makes its own effort through constant respiration of the body and thereby performs its own *jihad* until the final expiration. As complement to the respiration of the breath is the human aspiration to perform the inner *jihad* so as to awaken the higher consciousness for the Divine Reality as the spark of a higher spiritual consciousness and the very breath of the soul.

What matters is the condition of the soul; the world passes away. We are our bodies, but not just our bodies. We are our minds, but through our imagination and the life of the emotions, we are far more than our rational and cognitive thought. We have a heart that beats the pulse of life, but there is another, a forgotten heart worth remembering, which serves as the central focus of our being. From our faces a light shines forth if not a darkness, although we do not know precisely from whence it comes or where it will lead us. We cast shadows on the wall of the room, but tomorrow other shadows will be there to take our place.

What matters and what needs to matter is the identity of a life, the realization of a knowledge, the wisdom of an experience, and the virtue of a soul. What matters is that living and dying form the great parameters of human existence and nothing more. As we live, we are dying, and although we die, we will continue to live because of the continuity and immortality of the soul. What matters is to see the world for what it truly is and to know oneself in the light of an illuminating First Principle, without the soul in any way being compromised by the darkening perspective that is associated with this world of duality, ignorance, false hope, and faithlessness.

The message of the body lies in the mystery of its own transcendence, reflecting the capacity of the house to reflect the sanctuary of the home and the duty of the husk to protect the kernel. The message of the intelligence lies in the luminosity of its origin, a laser beam of intuition and insight that creates a trajectory for it to cut through the duality of the world in order to discern truth and reality from all falsehood and illusion. The message of the mind lies in the secret of human consciousness which overlays the intelligence with its prescience of spirit and its sacred awareness of self. The message of the heart lies in its intuitive capacity to feel what we know to be true, and thus to internalize that knowledge within the sanctuary of our being as the true modality of perception and free will. The message of the soul is that *we are not* what we appear to be in our existential reality; but that *we are* what we appear to be in our spiritual reality. We are finite beings whose bodies and all the accompanying faculties and fields of perception partake of death as the final act of transcendence that releases the soul from its finite bondage to live within the plenitude of the Infinite.

In principle, the human being is the perfected "I" and not the unfinished "I." We contain within our principial self the primordial man, the true man, the perfect man, and the universal man mentioned in the various spiritual traditions and not the animal soul that is the hidden disclosure of the modern theory of evolution. We are the perennial journeyers and seekers after truth. As journeyers, we live our inner life within a borderland: the outer limit of our body borders on the external world, while the inner limit of our soul borders on the world of the spirit. As seekers after truth, we become a gate of departure and return, the only such gate within the terrestrial world, which leads us out of the natural world of finitude into the supernatural world of the Supreme Self, the only world where the promise of the eternal life can be found, and where the true identity of the soul can be fully realized.

In view of the ensemble of the higher faculties, gathered together to serve as watchful sentinels of the mind—from the practicality of reason to the precision and clarity of the intelligence, from the primordiality of the spiritual instinct to the simple truthfulness of the emotions, from the holiness of the heart to the luminosity of the intellect—it is the soul that provides the foundation and ground for the intricate architecture of the inner person: soundless, solemn, sacred, and eternal. If you were to lift the veil of invisibility that surrounds the soul so as to reveal its true countenance, you may end up seeing a human face. The soul is the quintessence of every man, woman, and child at any given moment, summarizing across the open field of a life the mystery and miracle of the human person.

Part Three

♣

Forces of Spirituality

Chapter Seven

♣

The Light of Faith
in the Shadow of Modernity

From the invisible He made all things visible, Himself being invisible.
(2 Enoch 48:5)

For such [the faithful], He has written faith in their hearts and strengthened them with a spirit from Himself.
(Quran 58:22)

In Part One and Part Two of this work, we have focused on the
higher faculties of knowledge and their inner modes of perception
that make it possible for us as human beings to answer the questions
raised by the mysterious and challenging world in which we find
ourselves living. We will now shift our emphasis from considerations
of a sacred science of mind to some reflections on the forces of spirituality that are unleashed through the implementation of these
transcending gifts of God and their consequences on both the outer
and inner life of humanity. The first consequence to emerge from
the ability to discern, to know, to imagine, to experience, and to feel
the truth is none other than the impulse to have faith and believe
in a Divine Being. Through this leap of mind and heart, those with
faith take the first step that leads them beyond the confines of the
individual self by confirming their spiritual identity through an
instinctive faith in a Supreme Intelligence. It is a step that takes
them beyond the horizon of the cognitive mind and opens the way
to the experience of the Infinite.

Perhaps nothing highlights more effectively the vast chasm that
exists between the traditional and modern worldviews than the
irrevocable differences that exist between the traditional and modern understanding of the concept of faith. A faith that can move
mountains in the traditional world is considered to be blind, naïve,
and sentimental in the modern world. A faith that unites sacred sentiment with the essential knowledge of God in the traditional world

is considered merely a blind assent or a whimsical desire in the modern world. In today's anti-spiritual environment, a prevailing faith in the validity of a surprising number of scientific principles remains unacknowledged by the scientific establishment. They refuse to admit that the ultimate ground of their first premises also represents a tenuous faith and insist on the pretence that nothing is true until proven with the human mind and bodily senses. How is it possible that the light of faith can mean so much to traditional society and so little to modern society?

Similarly, perhaps nothing defines more clearly the role of faith in the modern world than the importance it plays in both the realization of the traditional knowledge and the pursuit and acquisition of today's scientific knowledge. The modern, scientific elite denies outright the spiritual efficacy—indeed the legitimacy—of a traditional faith without realizing that they in fact rely on the instinct of faith to initiate a thought process that will lead to the kind of knowledge they desire to uncover. In the pursuit of either spiritual or scientific knowledge, faith must inevitably be the starting point in a thinking process that sinks its roots into an accepted knowledge. Whether it is in the traditional or the modern context, people inevitably rely upon a certain kind of faith to acquire a certain kind of knowledge. Under the circumstances, the concept of faith is a power pack of implications that both modern scientists and people generally cannot ignore unless they wish to deceive themselves.

One of the many dilemmas facing people today, and perhaps one that effectively highlights the perennial mystery that continues to underscore their entire existence, lies in the fact that they no longer know the meaning of traditional faith. Indeed, since the concept of faith during these times has been reduced to the level of a blind wish or a vague and sentimental aspiration, people no longer realize that the face of faith, as portrayed within the various spiritual traditions through the millennia, has many profiles and conveys, in addition to the knowledge of God, many sacred emotions that are both revealing and intimate.

Initially, faith exists as a natural predisposition within a person to explain the unexplainable and to bridge the chasm that exists between the sheer physicality of the human being and the phenomenal world on the one hand, and the invisibility of God and the spiritual world on the other. As part of our nature, we are never without some kernel of faith that eventually reveals the secret disposition of our inner self. In view of the crucial mystery that exists concerning our origin and true nature, faith manifests itself firstly as a purely abstract idea, a desire, a premonition that seizes the mind in order to confront the barrier of inscrutable mystery that we face with its broad avenue of possibility and hope. There arises in the mind the prospect of moving across the isthmus between known and unknown worlds in order to experience reality as a truth and not just as a speculation. Faith implies a choice and the believer says *yes* to the knowledge of the Absolute Reality and to the love of the Supreme Being that is expressed in sacred Revelation, revealed through the symbolic messages of Nature, and personified within our very being.

The face of faith shines as an initial spark of light that can illuminate our inner consciousness with the knowledge of God, partly because the knowledge of God resolves the mystery that surrounds our origin and true nature, and partly as an antidote to the darkness and uncertainty that the life of this world embodies when it is understood to be an independent reality of its own. What begins as a presentiment and grows into a ray of light ultimately becomes a burning conviction in which we commit ourselves to the principles of a sacred and essential knowledge that defines for us the nature of reality. Our imagination alone cannot reconcile the invisible and the visible, the metaphysical and the physical, the Creator and the creation; it is only through the illumination of the light of faith that the mind, heart, and soul can see the divine qualities within the visible, physical, and formal aspects of the creation by acknowledging the inner reality of things that are veiled and embedded within the invisible aspects of the creation.

Faith commences as a fundamental assertion to believe in a Divine Reality. It then stakes its claim within the mind and heart by setting forth a desire for a complete knowledge of reality that expresses a certainty and projects a truth. As such, faith is free of the constraints of the dogma and form contained in religion and lives as a purely personal and intimate condition of mind and heart. Faith establishes an attitude of mind that serves as the foundation and backdrop of a person's active spiritual life, lending meaning and purpose to all that life's experience contains. We can then face the existential reality of the world with the armor of a faith that predisposes us to the knowledge of God and to the efficacy of His guidance and mercy. Faith reveals its knowledge in proportion to the predisposition of the person to incorporate this faith into their life as an existential reality. As such, faith becomes a profile of all that is mysterious in life and gives definition to the divine mystery that lies at the heart of earthly existence.

Modern humanity expresses a profound ambivalence toward the concept of faith. It rejects the traditional faith of its ancestors by calling it blind, sentimental, and childish; at the same time, it considers faith a psychological impulse merely reflective of the fear of the unknown. The true meaning of faith, its power to move mountains and its significance as a gateway to a transcending, metaphysical knowledge, is lost. People today do not realize, for example, that faith serves as the instinctive motivation in the pursuit of a knowledge that can transcend worlds, that a fundamental faith forms the lodestone of all encounters with authentic knowledge, whether they be ancient, traditional, modern, or scientific, and that faith draws its energy from a source that is the Origin and Final End of all knowledge.

Behind the open face of faith lies the instinctive human impulse to reveal itself as either a spontaneous, holy affirmation or an inner impulse without a conscious origin. The pursuit and acquisition of knowledge begins as a fundamental faith that draws on the intelligence and the holy sentiments of the heart because "He has written faith in their hearts" and grows into a certainty because He has "strengthened them with a spirit from Himself" (Quran 58:22). The knowledge of faith allows traditional believers to see the invisible through the visible, rather than deny the Invisible solely on the evidence of the visible.

♣ ♣ ♣

The traditional worldview portrays faith as an instinct that transcends the limitations of this world by accepting a framework of knowledge and initiating an attitude of mind that gives shape and coloration to the entire thinking process. As such, faith has traditionally been recognized as the point of departure in the pursuit of a knowledge of self and the world that can be experienced as a reality, indeed as *the* Reality, even though such a reality is invisible and cannot be seen. In order to come to terms with the unseen reality that is the true reality, the impulse of faith has always aided traditional believers in accepting a body of knowledge that has descended from above, a knowledge that comes to humankind as a divine revelation, a knowledge that represents the actual word of the Divinity, a knowledge with the power to enlighten and save. Faith's desire constitutes the first step in a journey of discovery and fulfillment that is based on the knowledge of God. As such, it is a gateway into the frontiers of sacred knowledge and an open door to conscious spiritual experience.

In contrast, the modern, scientifically based worldview displays an ambivalent, if not paradoxical, attitude toward the mystery of faith; ambivalent because it also relies on a faith of sorts to proceed with its investigation, and paradoxical because faith assumes a belief in the unseen and that is precisely what the scientific mind sets out to disprove. The modern scientific establishment denies faith's power and efficacy; but at the same time its very *raison d'être* relies on a faith that has the ability to leap across vast chasms of theory and speculation in the pursuit of knowledge. Yet, the question arises: What kind of knowledge? Is the answer a speculative knowledge based on observation, experimentation, and precise mathematical formulae or a metaphysical knowledge based on revelation, the symbols of nature, and the faculty of the human intellect with its direct access to a higher knowledge? Is it knowledge based on a faith in human reason or a knowledge accessed through a transcending faith?

At the heart of the secularist worldview lies the doctrine that there is no reality but the physical reality and there is no absolute truth beyond what can be quantified and objectified by human reason and the corporeal senses. This is a primary example of a modern-day faith that every scientist asserts in the pursuit of the scientific mandate. To assert that nothing exists except a physical reality is purely arbitrary, theoretical, and ultimately imaginary. In such a worldview, there is no place for the aspirations of a traditional faith with its open invitation to cross frontiers, explore deep wildernesses, and leap across the isthmus between alien worlds in order to come to terms with the truth and the reality that underlies all existence. The modern secularist worldview is based on what amounts to an empty faith in the validity of speculative truths; there can be no omniscient Divinity, no absolute Reality, and no ultimate Truth to which traditional faith lays claim.

The difference between the role of traditional faith and the modern faith in scientific principles lies in their respective points of departure. Both starting-points are equally characterized by an unwavering faith in the validity of their assumed beliefs and both equally employ the human mind in making deductions from these starting-points. The kind of faith that characterizes the pursuit of knowledge during the modern era, however, is embedded within the scientific premises and hypotheses that jump-start the entire scientific pursuit of knowledge, while the faith of the traditional world is not only the point of departure in the pursuit of knowledge, it virtually defines all human spirituality. Without an instinctive and motivating faith in the unseen reality and without a firm belief in higher levels of consciousness and spiritual experience, there can be no knowledge of God, no religious path, no spiritual disciplines such as prayer and meditation, no true virtue, and ultimately no transcendence.

Faith presupposes a body of preliminary assumptions that amount to being assertions—whether they be metaphysical or merely physical and scientific—concerning the reality of Truth and the true nature of Reality. The faith embodied within these assumptions commences a line of thought that produces all kinds of deductions and leads toward a certain kind of knowledge that is in keeping with the original aspirations of faith. The faith of both the traditional and scientific worldviews represents a leap of the mind, a willingness and an affirmation of what one believes to be the categorical imperative of the mind, whether it be the Transcendent Reality or a purely physical reality. Beyond the initial leap of mind that bridges the distance between two alien worlds lies the framework of one's thinking, including the choices one brings to bear in the pursuit of a particularized knowledge and the examination of its evidence. Ultimately, each point of view determines the conclusions that are reached because of the initial faith in a particular framework of knowledge.

The traditional mind relies on a firm faith in the Transcendent Reality, which overlays the entire manifested creation as an Immanent Reality, and provides the seamless whole to a vast universe of infinite possibility as an Infinite Reality. As exemplary and definitive professions of faith, the *credo in unum Deum* of Christianity and the *la ilaha illa 'Llah* of Islam articulate the essence of the Absolute Truth and announce the impending reality of the Divine

Presence. What distinguishes traditional faith and defines its parameters is the belief in the unseen reality of the abiding Spirit as an inner, spiritual dimension that empowers and substantiates all aspects of the phenomenal world. The experience of faith turns the initial willingness to believe into certitude of the mind.

At the heart of faith's imperative lies the truth that humanity cannot encounter the Divinity directly. Traditional believers did not face the mystery implicit within the phenomenal world of the cosmos any more directly than they faced God directly or expected to see the Divine Countenance.[1] Traditional knowledge has come to humanity indirectly through enlightened messengers, through revelation, through nature, through symbols, and through human introspection,[2] and not directly between the Divine Being and the human being. The perception of the reality among people living in a traditional environment was synthetic rather than analytic; their understanding was based on a synthesis of knowledge, not just any knowledge of course, but the essential knowledge that unifies and saves. God enlightens human beings through essentially three sources of knowledge; they are Revelation, Nature, and the self as a prototype self-revelation,[3] and this creates the condition through which a symbolic and analogical understanding of the true nature of reality is possible.

Contrary to the popular perception which thinks that modern science is based solely on observation, experimentation, and clear reasoning leading to logical—and seemingly correct—conclusions, the scientific mind relies on none other than a kind of faith in substantiating its working principles. It commences its journey in search of the truth through a leap of mind into abstract and theoretical areas of thought that would otherwise be inaccessible. The primordial truths of modern scientific thought, namely their

---

1. The veil between the human and the Divine is absolute. Humans will therefore not see God, any more than Moses was able to see God, and Moses was a prophet. "'Oh Lord,' Moses said to God when he reached the appointed place. 'Show Thyself to me, that I may look upon Thee.' But God replied: 'By no means canst thou see Me directly'" (Quran 7:143).

2. "Know thyself in order to know God" (a traditional saying of the Prophet).

3. According to the Quran, there are three basic sources of knowledge. They are the knowledge within revelation, the symbols of nature, and the experience of the self. "Soon We will show them Our signs on the horizon and within themselves until it becomes clear to them that this is the Truth" (Quran 41:53).

assumptions, theories, and hypotheses, are not subject to the rigors of empirical or experimental verification; they are abstract, arbitrary, and purely hypothetical points of departure that lead the way in a particular line of reasoning.

There are a number of such articles of faith that are taken as axiomatic within the scientific community and are simply not challenged by members of the establishment, who would greatly risk being ostracized if they did. They include the belief that the structure of reality is purely mathematical, an assumption that constitutes virtually the cornerstone of the *credo* of the modern scientific worldview. Similarly, there is the abstract assumption and hypothetical search for unity underlying the phenomenal universe, which completely belies empirical or experimental verification. When asked what proof there was that nature possessed unity, Einstein replied *C'est un acte de foi* ("It is an act of faith"). Indeed, the very fact that scientists rely exclusively on either empirical evidence or mathematical formulae in order to identify an objective reality is itself a purely hypothetical assumption. Is sense data the definitive medium to establish objectivity? Are the principles of mathematics the sole criteria that can discriminate between what is true and what is false? If the answer to these valid questions is yes, then it begs the question: Who said so? The modern mentality may believe in sense data and mathematics, but what is the basis of this assumption and what is the source of its objectivity beyond the leap of mind required to establish and define these empirical norms?

In spite of the high visibility of the phenomenal world and the provability of the material world, people today still have no clear sense of the true nature of reality; they therefore have no idea of the true nature and consequences of their actions in such a mysterious and enigmatic world. Because the fundamental mystery of the creation refuses to give up its elemental secrets or betray its otherworldly mystique, a sense of certainty will continue to elude the modern mind unless it can achieve both authenticity and certainty through a transcending faith in a body of God-revealed knowledge. The modern scientific elite, who are the high priests of today's world and who alone have the power to speak *ex cathedra* on such questions as the nature of reality and the origin of life, have established the fundamental criteria concerning the true nature of reality and the human beings who inhabit that reality. They alone have the right to form the fundamental interrogatives that make up the parameters of the scientific inquiry.

In the scientific worldview, the post-modern individual is regarded as an autonomous, physical entity whose biological, chemical, and atomic properties expand beyond their natural parameters to cause subtle manifestations of thinking and feeling that are rooted exclusively within the physical world of matter. We exist as it were apart from God and apart from any kind of force that could be characterized as spiritual, otherworldly, or beatitudinal. We have not been created by God and we will not return to Him, in contradiction of the simple yet eloquent Quranic verse "We come from God and to Him we shall return" (2:152). We are thought of as being nothing more than individual and finite creatures that have their moment in time and will eventually disappear back into the energy of the cosmos—nothing more. We enjoy a faculty called reason, a faculty that is most notably cut off from both Revelation and the Intellect because these higher faculties relate to the supra-human level of reality that science denies. Yet modern sophisticates believe that the faculty of reason somehow illuminates the human mind through a light of its own making. Reason is a god because it is regarded as the sole instrument that can navigate its way through the sea of universal mystery and that can lead them to a destination they know not where. Anything that transcends the faculty of human reason is treated quite simply as nonverifiable knowledge, or worse, as the sub-product of an over-ripe and misguided imagination.[4]

The modern scientific worldview asserts that life, consciousness, and self-awareness are nothing but manifestations of complex

4. Some scientists would like to reduce the human species to its lowest common denominator and render it not much more profound than a distinctive group of well-oiled machines. The biologist Richard Dawkins, an aggressive proponent of numerous "evolutionary tales," has suggested in his book *The Selfish Gene* that we can think of ourselves as "survival machines," invented through evolutionary tinkering by ancient replications, snippets of DNA. In speaking of "genes," Dawkins has written: "Now they swarm in huge colonies safe inside gigantic lumbering robots, sealed off from the outside world, communicating with it by tortuous indirect routes, manipulating it by remote control. They are in you and in me; they created us, body and mind; and their preservation is the ultimate rationale for our existence" (Quoted in Douglas Hofstadter, *The Mind's Eye: Fantasies and Reflections on Self and Soul* [New York: Bantam Books, 1985], p. 131).

arrangements of inanimate particles that have evolved in a fortuitous way to result in the phenomenon called *Homo sapiens.* Modern science proclaims the existence of the phenomenal world as an independent reality that can be studied and known in an ultimate sense, without any reference to a higher order of reality and without cognizance of a universal Creator. Space, time, matter, motion, and energy establish the parameters of the physical world and are thus expressed and believed-in realities that are independent of any higher order of being and are cut off from the power and influence of a Supreme Being. The physical world is portrayed as a mechanical world subject to quantifiable mathematical laws. Anything within nature that does not fall within that rubric and is in essence non-quantifiable is irrelevant to the study of modern science. Faith in the veracity of these suppositions serves as the lodestar for modern civilization and as a guiding light for the evolving, modern worldview.

♣ ♣ ♣

"Blessed are they that have not seen and yet have believed" (John 20:29). This sacred saying of Christ has as much relevance today as it once had two thousand years ago. Perhaps we will find that the role of faith in the modern world is similar to the role of faith in the traditional world, at least from the spiritual point of view. Faith in the modern world can still provide the means of activating the spiritual emotions and bridging the gap that otherwise exists between the mind and the will, between our knowledge of the truth and what we are willing to act upon. Moreover, faith initiates a process of inner inquiry that offers a vision into the true nature of reality and permits people to develop and appreciate a sense of the sacred in all aspects of life.

Faith flows like a river through the being of the faithful person. It transcends both time and place by placing us within our own center and situating us within the eternal moment. Faith has the capacity to lift the veil of the Divine Mystery, to enliven the sacred traditions, and to overlay the symbolic image of the human being with a projection of the perfected being that we are destined to become.

As the point of departure for all spirituality, faith is both knowledge and belief. As knowledge, faith represents a modality of mind—an intuition if you will—that can awaken human spirituality by acknowledging the existence of an Absolute Being as the Origin and Source of everything in existence, including true believers who bring to faith its living consciousness. Faith as a basic intuition represents knowledge of a doctrine whose implicit blessing is the certitude that what we believe is the absolute truth. As a belief, faith represents a modality of will that activates our free will to believe in God, a Divinity who has created, sustains, and will ultimately save or damn our soul. As such, faith contains a power that transcends form, a power that can formalize the abstract into a clear image of the Divine, a power that can link outer and inner worlds like a bridge, and a power that can be a veil to protect as well as a key to unlock the dam of spiritual forces that lies at the center of our being.

Because faith amounts to being a human intuition based on knowledge of the Divine and a desire to turn toward God, it has the potential to become a force that can move mountains, that permits the faithful to manifest inner realities through visible actions, that reduces the great impasse that exists between matter and spirit to a modern myth, and that shatters the mirror of all earthly illusions and actually begins the process of lifting the veil of all the cosmic mysteries.[5] Ultimately, faith has the power to raise the human soul onto the plane of immanent and eternal realities.

Faith has once again become a force too powerful to be denied by the modern men and women of our time and its significance and implications are too subtle to be summarily rejected or ignored by modern sophisticates. Faith, within the context of the modern world, can no longer be labeled as merely psychological or blind and dismissed by those who deny its possibilities as appropriate only for children, sentimentalists, arcane spiritualists, and possibly fools, as though the perennial faith of millions from time immemorial could be passed off by more mature modern minds as a human need to believe in fairy tales.

Faithless men and women of this age have the tendency to explain faith's dynamic range as being the mere childishness or sentimentalism of people with no desire to think, as if the cerebral thinking of modern times could replace faith's range and depth.

---

5. "The veil is a notion which evokes the idea of mystery, because it hides from view something that is either too sacred or too intimate; but it also enfolds a mystery within its own nature when it becomes the symbol of universal veiling" (Frithjof Schuon, *Esoterism as Principle and as Way* [Pates Manor, Bedfont: Perennial Books, 1981], p. 47).

When faith is not passed off as a thoughtless sentimentality, it is then labeled as blind—a pejorative word intended to imply that it is nothing more than a sightless vision, or the infamous believing without seeing scorned by the scientific community, founded upon a human psychology that needs faith to explain the unknown nature of reality. Simple human psychology suggests, however, that we need faith, not as a childish alternative for a frightened and unsophisticated psyche, but rather as a pragmatic approach to the unknown, in which our thoughts, emotions, and actions are empowered by the knowledge of God that accompanies faith.

The secret of faith, however, lies beyond the thinking mind. Down through the ages people have always been faced with a number of unknown factors that demand of the thinking mind a faith either in the existence of a Supreme Intelligence who creates, guides, and sustains their lives or a faith in some credible alternative, what in modern times would amount to a belief in the verity of an evolutionary process that originates somewhere—anywhere—and proceeds along a path of natural selection and survival of the fittest, which ultimately promises a human progress that will eventually bring modern humanity to a superhuman condition, if not an enlightened state of being.

The modern day alternative to faith is nothing short of a faith in religion's counterpart: a faith in modern science that is based on human reason rather than divine revelation. People during these times cannot escape the impulse of a faith in something—anything—since the unknown factors that continue to haunt the modern psyche force people to retain a faith, if not in God, then in the evolutionary process, for neither are provable according to the demands of scientific scrutiny[6] and both require faith with its implicit leap of mind and its broad demands on the imagination. With regard to such an initiating faith, the theory of evolution is

6. We refer here to the macro-evolutionary process for which there is not a single piece of hard evidence to document its existence. Micro-evolutionary processes, on the other hand, are well documented and not in doubt. "Darwin himself had increasing doubts as to the validity of his views, and the only aspect of his theory which has received any support over the past century is where it applies to micro-evolutionary phenomena. His general theory . . . is still, as it was in Darwin's time, a highly speculative hypothesis entirely without direct factual support and very far from the self-evident axiom some of its more aggressive advocates would have us believe" (Michael Denton, *Evolution: A Theory in Crisis*, p. 77).

no different from religion, as much as modern scientists hate to admit it.

In fact, in today's world any personal commitment to faith can be reduced to the level of sheer incredibility. For example, is it more incredible to believe in God as Divine Being and Supreme Intelligence than to believe in an evolutionary process in which the human body actually evolved after a complex progression of chance and accidental factors, beginning with chemicals in a pre-biotic process of evolution, and which somehow combined to form a complex grouping of molecules that ultimately became a living cell that built itself into a thinking creature with a consciousness of self? Is it more incredible to believe that humanity is made in the image of God with a human consciousness of self, a consciousness that can be raised to a height of purity of mind with a pristine clarity that forms the basis of a potential ennoblement? Isn't it more incredible that human consciousness has somehow derived from matter and that it is a sophisticated, refined or somehow highly evolved form of matter?

Perhaps the worldly-wise people of today should approach the mystery of faith from the possibilities inherent in these levels of incredibility in order to cross the barrier that continues to exist between faith and disbelief. Only then will they be able to arrive at a satisfactory answer to the contemporary challenge to the efficacy of traditional faith, a challenge that proposes the unbelievable and unreal hypotheses that the higher has evolved from the lower, that consciousness has emerged out of the elements of subatomic particles, that life has burst forth spontaneously from matter, and that matter itself could serve as the benchmark and basis of an objective reality.

♣ ♣ ♣

Faith is the formal bridge between inviolate worlds: between matter and spirit, body and soul, outer and inner modalities, earthly and celestial realities. As such, faith brings together these two antithetic realities and makes possible the meeting of the human and the Divine.

Firstly, faith strikes down the absolute barrier that exists between matter and spirit with its wand of inspiration and insight. Through a body of revealed knowledge to inspire the mind and through a holy yearning of the heart to activate that knowledge, faith bridges the vast distance that separates us from the Sublime. The sacred intuition of faith permits an understanding of unity to be possible between the world of form and the world of spirit, each realm influencing the other in an interactive and harmonious blending of earthly and celestial realities. Because of faith, the physicality of the world of matter does not pre-empt our perception of reality with its dense materiality. Instead the phenomenal world can serve as a symbol of a high knowledge and visualize for us a higher reality. Faith allows the believer to understand, if not actually see, the forces of spirit at work within matter. The world of nature is the prime example of form virtually glowing with spirit.

Secondly, faith bridges the great divide that exists between the cognitive mind and the intelligent heart, as much as between the intelligent heart and the abiding Spirit. This divide exists on existential levels in which we understand ourselves to be living beings without explanation and fragmented beings that are a mysterious as well as a physical reality. It is as if we project two personalities out of ourselves: an outer persona manifested in the ego, which responds to the demands of our body and its immediate environment; and an inner persona that lies further within us and runs as a deep undercurrent that emerges at moments in life when we are able to discard our worldly presumptions and preconceived attitudes for a spiritual intuition that projects the best of our inner selves into the outer world of people and forms.

Thirdly, in its mediatory function as a bridge to inner worlds, faith is at home within the borderland of the spirit. It sets in motion a movement of the spirit that must be activated as part of the spiritual challenge of our time; otherwise it will lie dormant deep within the inner sanctum of the being and never surface to illuminate the mind and heart. Through a traditional faith made contemporary by virtue of its timely aspiration, a process of spirituality can begin once again that can make faith a coloration of the soul in which believers prepare themselves, stand firm, open their being, and put themselves on the line as it were for the discovery of that which cannot be explained in words, but which can create a music of the spirit, a bow on strings, that can articulate for us the greatest truth of which we are capable. Faith permits, indeed begins, a dialogue between ourselves and the Divine Being, whether He be identified as the Hindu Brahma, the Christian God the Father, the Jewish YHVH, the Islamic Allah, or the Great Spirit of the North American Indians, permitting a clarity of mind, a melting of the heart, and an opening of the soul toward the Spirit through the music of our own being.

Finally, through faith, individual humans assent to their insignificance in the face of the Absolute Being. Based on revelation and activated through intuition, faith is above all the humble acknowledgement of our place within the cosmic design of the Supreme Intelligence. We need faith as compensation to the unknown mystery and as the key to the knowledge of the unseen reality. Perhaps the time has come, as we cross the threshold into the new millennium and face a different set of demands that will be inevitable in the 21st century, to abandon our earthly pretensions and adopt once again the humble attitude of faith as the necessary prelude to unknown realms of knowledge and as the instinctive motive in activating a life of contemporary spirituality?

We need to approach one another as human beings once again. We need to abandon the superficial mask of our false, modern persona that now believes in a process of evolution that actually separates people from each other with its neutral, amoral philosophy of natural selection and survival of the fittest, instead of bringing them together with a unified and credible worldview. We need to find a deeper expression of self that is based on the eternal verities and modeled by the great prophets, saints, and mystics of recorded history, an expression of spirituality that makes the invisible visible by virtue of the heart and soul invested in humanity by the Divinity. Perhaps we can meet each other once again, not based on a superficial knowledge of matter and form, but on the basis of a faith in a knowledge that transcends the physical plane to reveal mysteries to which we would not otherwise have access. Perhaps we can meet each other out of a knowledge that we have truly experienced and suffered and come to realize, a knowledge that inspires a human commitment to transcend our limitations in ways that only faith in the knowledge of God permits.

If faith is to survive in the modern world as a spiritual force that is a viable option for the modern mentality, several important factors need to be realized. Firstly, contemporary humanity must abandon its preconceived notions about faith, notions that have accumulated over the centuries and have now solidified into an attitude that is both negative and counterproductive, not to mention misleading and false. Secondly, with regard to the dynamic spiritual force that faith contains, the mind must become once again a *tabula rasa*, in which all mental projections, preconceived opinions, and unwarranted prejudices can be abandoned for the motivating impulse of faith, whose power and insight can unlock inner doors of perception and higher levels of awareness with the ability to reorder the way in which the mind perceives and processes the modern experience. Finally, people today must realize what they are in their essence: not the spiritual dwarf that now constitutes the portrait of *Homo modernus,* but the human image in reflection of the Supreme Being and the *homo spiritualis* portrayed in sacred scripture.

A faith based on the revelatory knowledge of God can become the vehicle of a legitimate interaction among people because it communicates not only facts and statistics, but also part of the essence of the person who passes it on, and because it conveys a sublime and absolute truth that far exceeds the implications of the physical world of matter. Such a faith would represent a knowledge that contains the fragrance of primordial meaning that once existed at the heart of the world and that still lies dormant somewhere near the horizon of our time.

Needless to say, there can be no spirituality without faith—modern, contemporary, traditional, or otherwise. Faith can be modern insofar as it exists during these times and takes into account the dynamic range of the newly emerging 21st century mentality. Faith can be traditional when it is based on a revealed knowledge that alone has the orthodoxy and the divine power to enlighten and save.

Our sacred duty during these times is to activate the revealed knowledge of the religions with the spiritual forces that exist within us through our intuition of God and our faith in the power to transcend our own limitations with that knowledge. A formal, traditional religion can become once again a living contemporary religion, just as a traditional society and culture can become a contemporary society and culture and still retain a traditional coloration that preserves a heightened consciousness and a firm will power made possible through the light of faith and the orthodoxy of the religious traditions.

The full expression of human spirituality can humanize the face of a religious tradition because the behavior and actions of the faithful give evidence of a higher reality; similarly a religious tradition can activate the spiritual forces latent within human beings in order to spiritualize their faces with the knowledge and light of God as a living experience.

Chapter Eight

♣

The Paradox of Free Will
and Fated Choices

It hath been taught us from the primal state
That he which is was wished until he were.
(Shakespeare, Antony and Cleopatra.)

According to all the great spiritual traditions of the world, the defining characteristic of the human species is the quality of human-ness, for want of a better term. Humanity is considered human because it enjoys a number of higher faculties that distinguish the species from the rest of the animal kingdom and place it at the pinnacle of the creation as a being created in the image[1] of God.

These faculties inhabit a borderland within our inner world that permit us to address the dual nature of the world that confronts us with presence of mind and navigate our way through the labyrinthine journey that eventually becomes the course of a life. Our reasoning represents a logical and rational continuum of our cognitive mind; our intelligence reflects the discerning luminosity of a higher illumination; our heart generates sentiment and feeling; our natural and spiritual instincts respond to an inborn knowledge; our emotions qualify our conscious world and shape its subjective texture and ambiance; our imagination follows the impulses of our creative mind and its natural curiosity opens the door of the Infinite. Ultimately, the soul gathers the activity of all these modalities and buries their consequences into the ground of our being as a summary statement of who we are. One last faculty remains to be identified, without which none of the other faculties could adequately function or find their way. This is the faculty of action, direction, and movement, what all the religions unanimously identify, not as a human will unbounded by

1. An image not necessarily in the sense of a pictorial form but in the sense of a reflection or shadow. Since God is not a form but a Spirit, any likeness or symbolic image must refer to God's inner qualities and attributes rather than to any physical properties.

any qualifying adjective, but as a human will set free to roam within the constraints the Creator has established for humanity.

The qualifying adjective "free" is crucial to the discussion. Of all the faculties and modes of perception that we have reflected upon in this work, perhaps the most controversial and problematic is the concept of free will. Down through the millennia, religious scholars and philosophers have engaged themselves with the paradox of free will, which functions as a faculty of the human being whose destiny was written before he or she were born and in a world that has been preordained down to the smallest grain of sand by the Divine Being. Every appearance seems to indicate to the modern mind that the faculty of willing is not free within the traditional perspective, at least at the surface level of appearances where the modern scientific establishment stakes its claim in the pursuit of what is real. It is a paradox that today's scientists love to highlight in their attempt to discredit the spiritual point of view. How can a person possess a will that is free, many modern-day skeptics like to ask, when everything is written in advance and the destiny of humanity is cast from a divine mold and predestined from eternity?

Admittedly, the approach to the problem of free will from the perspective of an earthly mentality will undoubtedly differ greatly from the panoramic view of the Divine Mind who presides from a metacosmic eternity outside the dimensional universe of time and space. We do not intend to recapitulate the arguments concerning free will and predestination for they have been explored with a thoroughness that should satisfy the most intransigent skeptic, mostly without resolution and to no avail. Whether the will is free or not may be a concern for those who like to argue about such things. It is a kind of modern-day existential semantic used by dissenters who love to play with words at the expense of the profound meaning they contain. In essence, the concept of free will is a spiritual paradox that finds its resolution in the power of its own reality and in the mystery of its own fulfillment. Perhaps we need to transcend the problem of free will rather than attempt to rationalize our way through its paradoxical implications merely as an effort to justify the contemporary predilection for denying God and anything associated with the world of the spirit.

Like a Japanese *koan*, free will is in principle an enigmatic and contradictory human faculty and a force of action that contains the seeds of an enlightenment whose existence cannot be denied and whose meaning will reveal itself and become known through the strength of its decision-making and the consequences of its execution. Like a traditional symbol, it has the power to reveal its meaning at a glance, through common sense, and through the force of its self-evident quality.

To that end, we need only ask ourselves what human behavior would be able to accomplish if its beloved will were not free. The answer would be as absurd as the question is fantastic. If humanity did not have the faculty of free will and therefore the means to put into effect that which the mind had construed, the logic of a rational mind demands that it would be acting under some kind of constraint rather than freely, like a chained animal or a caged bird, whereas the image of a free flying bird is a symbol if ever there was one of the unbounded soul. Even the wind "bloweth where it listeth." In such a strange scenario as the human experience bounded by a pre-determined destiny and without the beatitude of a free will as the empowering complement to a conscious mind, the word liberty would not even be part of the lexicon, much less form the basis of the human self-image! On the other hand, to say that humans have free will does not mean to imply that they enjoy absolute freedom in the sense that people today would like to imagine as part of the bold fantasy of their self-image, namely as a complete and total freedom, like some kind of god.

The kind of freedom that the modern psyche envisages for itself would actually make no sense on the human level and for obvious reasons: If people were not determined in some manner and could assume the mantle of a complete freedom, as many modern sophisticates would like to believe, then they could make themselves into whatever image they wanted. Individuals could change their race, color, or station in life according to their will; and yet this is clearly not within the realm of human possibility. It is a spiritual as well as an existential impossibility and one that no sane person would attempt to deny. On the contrary, we are predestined to be born within a certain condition of time and place and nothing, and especially no amount of desire or wanting, can change that fact. As Frithjof Schuon has noted: "The truth lies between the two extremes, or between two absurdities."[2] We must deal with the

2. Frithjof Schuon, *Stations of Wisdom* (London: John Murray, 1961), p. 81.

existential reality of our destiny and can do so with the faculty of a free will that can put into motion and give direction to the impulses of our mind, without pretending to aspire to the kind of absolute freedom that would place us beyond the need to eventually give an accounting of ourselves before our Maker.

Differences of perspective between the traditional and modern attitudes toward free will and the true nature of our freedom lie in a proper understanding of human limits and in the recognition of certain realities about the human being. Human limits defer to the nature of human destiny in which a person understands that they will never be able to alter certain parameters of their existence, namely the condition and circumstances into which they are born such as their race, color, birth date, or the genetic makeup of their DNA. Still, those limits contain a liberating, as well as a demanding, reality, in which an individual not only has the right and the freedom to make their own individual choices during the course of their life, but also the duty to meet the moment with the truth that every moment demands. Humility demands that we acknowledge certain realities, while intelligence allows us to know our place within the course of an individual destiny and to fulfill the role in which we find ourselves with equanimity and grace.

Does God know the destiny of an individual soul? Only a human being could have the temerity to ask such a question. The answer must be and is in the affirmative since God is omniscient and knows all things, otherwise He would not be God. Does God's knowledge somehow compromise our free will and our ability to choose? The answer must be and is a resounding no since a predestined and discretionary knowledge that exists outside the envelope of time and space has no affect whatsoever on the power of an individual will and the force of its action. What makes the difference in understanding this seemingly opaque paradox is the point of view and the angle of vision. "Man is subject to predestination because he is not God, but he is free because he is made 'in the image of God.' God alone is absolute freedom, but human freedom . . . is not something other than freedom any more than a feeble light is something other than light."[3]

3. Frithjof Schuon, *Understanding Islam* (Bloomington, IN: World Wisdom Books, 1994), p. 2.

God's knowledge may appear to fully compromise individual decision-making because it seems to cast an aura of predestination over our life insofar as He knows what will happen. From the divine point of view, however, the knowledge of God does not precede or predestine humanity any more than God Himself can be cast into the envelope of the universe He Himself has created. He is beyond time and space and as such He is called the All-Encompassing One (*al-Wasi*) in Islam as well as the All-Knowing and the Omniscient One (*al-'Alim*). Much of the discussion concerning the paradox of free will virtually hinges on points of view and terms of reference.

From the human point of view no one can take our freedom of choice away from us, least of all the All-Possibility of a Supreme Being who has bestowed upon His thinking creation the power to create a life of their own making to the extent that they will be called upon to give an accounting of their intentions and actions on the Day of Accounting. God's knowledge does not touch upon or compromise in any way the human thinking process and the unquestioned force of the will. If it did, there could be no question of responsibility within the theater of human actions and no question of an accounting either during or at the end of life.

Free will is real and not compromised by the knowledge of God, otherwise it could not take part in the existential reality of this world, nor could it take a decision and act upon it in a manner that goes contrary to the knowledge of God. The proof that the will is free, if proof be needed, lies in the fact that humanity can deny the very existence of the Divinity, as well as the knowledge and grace that are the evident manifestations of a Supreme Being. What could be more characteristic of the principle of freedom than the ability to affirm or deny the very origin and source of human existence?

The significance of free will takes on an added dimension within the intellectual climate of the modern world, partly because people have never before denied the existence of a Supreme Being to the extent that they do today in virtually every aspect of life, and partly because people have never before taken such a vested interest in searching for the clues to their own identity within such a narrow scope of self inquiry, limited that is to the purely physical plane of existence. Perhaps it is the folly of the modern mentality thoroughly adapted to the secular ambiance of the scientific worldview; but in this post-modern era, the society itself is forever scrutinizing and redefining itself, questioning and probing, especially now in light of the astounding findings of modern biology and physics down to the smallest quantum detail, in an effort to find an answer to life's mystery and particularly the mystery of the self, a search that will be arrived at on its own terms and will suit the demands of its mentality. There is danger as well as wisdom in such self-scrutiny, a kind of modern-day paradox that serves as a mirror image to complement the paradox of free will that has haunted the mind of humanity down through the ages.

Unlike lower creatures who act without question and are locked within the safety of their own particular natures, people today think they possess a kind of freedom without restraint but whose true nature and meaning is as enigmatic and challenging as the debatable freedom portrayed in the traditional paradox of free will. Awash in the wave of modernity, people follow the lead of scientists who define the meaning of the human being and write their own conception of self based on the findings of the various fields of modern science such as biology, chemistry, and paleontology. Members of the scientific establishment search within the depths of the physical entity and probe the vast expanse of the universe for answers to the abiding questions of our time; they have the stamina, determination, and freedom to do as they like within the must-resolve and can-do ambiance prevalent in the world of research and development. Indeed, the luxury of a perceived freedom and its liberating quality is perhaps the greatest feature creating a sense of progress within the contemporary setting. In short, the supposedly expanded and liberated mind of today, both among scientists and laypersons, attempts to see things purely from the human point of view, whereas the traditional mentality was accustomed to seeing things from the revelatory point of view in which the self-disclosure of God established the norm and set the prerogative for the faithful to follow. Perhaps the greatest paradox of all in today's world is the human perception of a liberating freedom that is based on the narrowest and most delimiting approach imaginable to the understanding of the true nature of reality.

In addition, the concept of an unlimited freedom because of the lowering of the threshold of accountability brought on by the modern-day denial of the Day of Judgment creates more problems than it eliminates and raises more questions than it resolves. What, for example, is the object of such freedom, in what direction does it lead us, and to what end will it bring us? These are ominous questions indeed that strike at the heart of the modern approach to ethics and morality, not to mention concerns about identity, purpose, and final end. Will this intense desire for answers the freedom it engenders give wing to a perennial search for the knowledge of the individual self, or will post-modern individuals eventually realize that the identity of the true inner person has taken on a coloration that is in fact infra-human and more bestial than any of the lower animals, who merely obey their predetermined nature and live harmoniously by using the God-given instincts to function naturally and harmoniously within the phenomenal world.

We are not speaking of the ideal image of humanity identified in the various traditions, the "true man" (*chen jen*) and "transcendent man" (*chün jen*) of the Taoist tradition or the "perfect" and "universal man" (*al-insan al-kamil*) of the Islamic tradition. Instead we are referring to the "unfinished person" that we now encounter within ourselves. From an evolutionary point of view, there is an unfinished aspect to the people living in today's modern societies that comes from the way they understand themselves. We are unfinished beings in a manner of speaking, incomplete and in search of a conception of self that has the explanatory power to meet the requirements of our true nature and fulfill the demands of our deepest desires. The great danger and perhaps the source of the greatest terror that confronts people today lies in the fact that the modern prototype does not know who or what it is and has not convincingly identified itself through the various fields of modern science. We as representatives of a so-called modern ideology seek but do not find; we witness but do not know who it is precisely that witnesses innerly; we knock, but the door to the intriguing mysteries of the universe does not open.

The darkest problem the person living today within a modern secular society faces is the inability to articulate a rationale of human identity and meaning that is the natural consequence of the seeds embedded within the ground of the modern scientific endeavor. Indeed the modern scientific endeavor does not embrace questions of identity and purpose. A comprehensive and intelligible definition of the human being does not exist during these times and cannot be drawn from the theories and discoveries of science because its false assumptions concerning the true nature of objectivity and the validity of the scientific method has created a closed system that attempts to operate within an open-ended universe. It is a case of the flee examining the elephant.

♣ ♣ ♣

In today's rarefied environment of confusion and ignorance, devotees of the scientific worldview know they have existence; but they do not know the ultimate source of this existence, not because they have not been told through the descent of a divine revelation in the various religious traditions, but because they do not accept other-worldly sources of knowledge, which they cannot prove on their own terms. In their attempt to fashion a projection of the human prototype within the modern scientific worldview, scientists have analyzed biological life down to the microscopic level of the cell where they have inadvertently discovered a micro-universe of astounding complexity, but they still do not know its origin or understand the complex mechanism of its functioning and development. This human image, not of God's making but rather of sheer form existing by chance and for its own sake, has an atomic constituency hovering on the brink of an indeterminacy that leaves it bereft of the solid matter that forms the basis and objectivity of its world. In truth, this "human image" has an existential profile of knowledge without certainty, reason without an illuminating guidance, faith in cosmic solitude and a set of faculties that substantiate truth and reality on its own terms and without the objectifying quality that accompanies the certitude of the Absolute. This human image enjoys a sense of freedom unfettered by the strictures of the traditional world; but at the expense of establishing a sufficient cause or providing a clear purpose or sense of direction.

By virtue of this unhampered freedom, people today wish and desire themselves to become a part of an existential reality that echoes the voice of the poet Shakespeare who wrote with his customary wisdom and insight: "He which is was wished until he were."[4] Many centuries ago, the famous bard suggested a truth, giving voice to an idea that people have known all along in their hearts, namely

4. William Shakespeare, *Antony and Cleopatra* (I, iv, 42).

that free will is a perennial problem that simply will not go away. What people wish for will come, what they want they will receive and what they desire to be, they will become, thereby creating in the process a free will prone to fatal choices with inescapable consequences. We can speculate and rationalize ourselves away until the sun shines at midnight, but we set ourselves in motion through the impulses of the will without knowing what vibrations will pass into ourselves and the world from what we say and do. What we wish will come; what we are we wished until it was.

This is not a spiritual paradox of ancient and traditional times but the stuff of a contemporary dilemma, creating for modern humanity a "politics of desire" that puts the people of today on the line in a manner that is not to their liking and is far beyond their control. There is nothing more dangerous to the quality of freedom and the luxury of desire than to receive what you want only to discover that you may not want it after all, reflecting a wanting that has no firm basis in a lasting knowledge and a desire that has no clear origin or valid justification. It is a perennial dilemma in which people know the subject of their desire without knowing its true object. They know what they want, but they do not know its true origin and its ultimate objective, namely what it is based on, what it should bring them, and why.

From where does a given desire emerge? It is a question worth asking, particularly during this time of unlimited and conflicting desire, since the impulse to have possessions and position and fame such as we have a mania for in today's world must inevitably bring its own consequences. To where does a given desire lead? No one can say for sure. A desire, however, once seized upon and committed to, brings us to the dilemma of inescapable choices, whose path, once taken, may lead in directions, not based on a knowledge that conforms to the light of the human intellect and sewn into the fabric of a life through reason and intelligence, but based on the indiscriminate urges of random wanting and biased choosing and far from the object of our true desire.

♣ ♣ ♣

One of the major, paradoxical mysteries of the self is not whether our will is free, but rather whether the will, being free in principle, can act within a framework that is enlarging from the individual point of view, but limiting from the metaphysical point of view. The question is not whether the will exists as unfettered and free, but more importantly what the source of that freedom is, and what it means to act freely. What would it mean to be deprived of the freedom to choose such as we find in the instinctive will of animals who praise God in following their instincts, and to act as one wills such as human beings enjoy as part of the human condition.

When we think of the faculty of human intelligence, we think of an enlightening knowledge, a cognitive, thinking mind, and a discerning and logical reason that through classification and analysis responds to the knowledge that comes to it from another, either a higher or a lower, source. The mind can generate an idea, glimpse a truth, perceive an illumination, and witness itself and all its endeavors through the awareness of self. When we think of the faculty of the will, we think of an incredible power to put into action the contents of the mind and a relentless force that molds and shapes the character and personality of the being. The free will virtually creates an individual character and an inner world.

Like Emerson who wrote, "The will constitutes the man," John Stuart Mill suggested that human character is the result of "a completely fashioned will."[5] He did not mean a medley of wills or a parade of ambitions and desires, but pure and unadulterated will, as in the raw uncorrupted power to put into effect what the mind has originated as a thought. He wrote of a universal will reflecting a unity of aim and a purposeful design that originates within and moves outward in a way that is as astounding as it is mysterious, a will that originates from within and creates the character of a person as he or she consciously intends themselves to be and as they were intended to be through the Supreme Will of a Divine Being. Through free will, the human being can become what it was intended to be under the circumstances into which it was born and in keeping with the characteristics of its individual nature and the limitations of its fundamental desires.

The individual will is primarily a reflection of the universal will in which the object of desire is drawn from within the primal urge

---

5. Quoted in James Hillman, *The Force of Character: And the Lasting Life* (New York: Ballantine Books, 2000), p. 175.

toward a universal principle, such as the desire for objectivity, for the absolute, for certainty, for happiness and fulfillment. Such willing is not inspired by random desire alone; it has universal characteristics and qualities and is inspired by the truth and not by the immediate interests of the ego. The will is universal when it takes part in a reality that is concentric rather than individual and transcends the contingencies of human desire. Like all the human faculties in their relation to universal principles, such as the mind as a reflection of the Mind of God or human consciousness mirroring the Universal Consciousness, the faculty of the will is universal when it is based on a universal principle that finds its source in the supreme Will of the Divinity.

The descriptions of modern science make no attempt to deal with the force and implications, not to mention the consequences, of free will. The issues of biology, chemistry, and even psychology are peripheral rather than central to human significance and deal with superficial modifications of the human body. The sciences have managed to take us apart without putting us back together again in an effort to describe us from the outside rather than attempting to define what we should be or how we might change from within, on the level of a luminous, discerning mind and a powerful free will. Judging from the sweeping advances in molecular biology and genetics, it may not be long before we will be building minds and hearts just as today we build buildings and cars. But who is the person and from where will the skill come to recreate the luminosity of a mind and the power of a free will such as humanity has in principle, a mind and a will that finds its source and meaning in the Mind and Will of a Supreme Divinity?

What has always interested people of both traditional and modern times is the full deployment of human possibilities that have as their consequence the utilization of the will resulting in the potential, life-long happiness of every individual on earth. Yet the implementation of the will and its underlying motive of human happiness must inevitably depend on the harmonious interaction of the intelligence, emotions, imagination, and thereafter the will and all that it implements and sends forth into the world.

There is a reciprocal relationship between intelligence and free will to the extent that the thoughts of the intelligence ultimately depend on the actions of free will; otherwise, they will lie dormant within the mind as wishful thinking, while the will transforms selected thought into effective action. Concerning the mind, we have already noted that to know one's mind requires knowledge of the true nature of the inner self, a knowledge without which the mind would be adrift like a great ocean liner in a sea of uncertainty and ignorance. Similarly, our free will does not consist in doing what we like or in doing what we must by the force of some natural compulsion; instead, it must also be guided by a higher knowledge of principles that permits the will to negotiate its way through the duality and vicissitudes of life in the world. The mind and will interact in multitudinous ways to make possible the felicity, the satisfaction, and the fulfillment of the human destiny.

Intelligence, with the support of the emotions and the imagination, precedes the impulse to will and provides the motivation to will a thing and make it happen. In much the same way that knowledge precedes faith and sustains, with its intellective nectar, faith's fervor and its force, knowledge fuels the mind with the will to act according to the contents of a conscious desire and can do so to the extent that the will is free to act and sufficiently strong to make the desire happen.

Yet the question returns to haunt us: How do we choose in life? We have many desires in the course of our life, including success, fulfillment, the attainment of the full range of qualities and virtues; all of these desires are based on a knowledge that certain things are worth fighting for and having. Obviously, the actualization of knowledge-cum-desire through the faculty of a free will depends to a large degree upon the human effort to bring it about. That is why the strength of the will is often alluded to in the various traditions; it is not enough that the will be free, it must also exhibit a strength of purpose and a fixed design in order to bring about a given desire and make it a reality. The mind exhibits a mindfulness that is silent witness to the movements of our thoughts and feelings, but the will emerges from another level of mind and represents a power to act from the living center of the being.

This leads us to make mention of the inherent dangers that all freedom imposes. In spite of the liberating quality that freedom grants to every individual, freedom also bears certain responsibilities and its own logical consequences. It carries with it a price in terms of presence of mind and individual effort that can often be very high. Being free, we may choose to follow the straight path and develop ourselves in a positive manner that actualizes the qualities and virtues that we want our character to exhibit. Being weak-willed, however, we may choose that which is contrary to either our immediate or ultimate interest and lead us in a direction that is actually contrary to our conscious desire. In fact, desire itself is a double-edged sword and can lead to our destruction when it is based on a knowledge and an impulse that leads to our willing the wrong thing.

We wrote earlier that faith anticipates the entire body of truth through a knowledge that a person is willing to affirm because of an active faith. Faith is an attachment to God and to the truth of God's existence as the one Reality. The impulse of faith may commence as a state of mind based on a higher knowledge, but free will puts faith into action so as to create an attachment to God that reaches down into the very core of the human being as an act of transcendence. The will participates in this faith and the knowledge it presupposes by making choices between truth and falsehood, between knowledge and ignorance, between good and evil. We are no stranger to these choices. Just as traditional peoples were well aware of the imposing duality of good and evil within the world, we as modern individuals know that the world entails good and evil, justice and injustice, knowledge and ignorance, and we cannot, and most of us do not, pretend otherwise, if only as a manner of humanistic sensibility. One major difference between the traditional and modern worlds lies in the perception and understanding of free will, how it should be implemented and to what end.

The reality of the choice of evil within this world cannot be denied by either the traditional or modern mentality, for its face within the world, particularly the modern world, is far too visible and far too apparent to be ignored or denied. The duality of good and evil, knowledge and ignorance, strength and weakness, perfection and imperfection, is an existential reality as well as a spiritual fact that needs to be recognized for what it is. The paradigm of the duality and split image of the human mind is contained in every thought, every action, every time, and every place. It is called the truth of the moment and the veracity of our place in time. When we desire a thing, we know in our heart of hearts that its choice can lead us in two opposing directions and that we cannot escape the consequences of what we implement through the force of our will and what we choose to desire.

It is not without reason that the traditions have always insisted upon the surrender of the human will to the Divine Will. It is an underlying principle of every religion for the very reason that every choice that is made and every moment that occurs contains a truth and a falsehood, a good and an evil, a denial and an affirmation within its earthly parameters; it is in the very nature of the world and a part of the fundamental challenge of a will that is free. That having been said, it should not be forgotten that the human will has the tendency toward the absolute Good because of its association with the knowledge of God. The essence of the will and its primary function is to choose the good, participate in the divine affirmation, and avoid negative consequences. That is the essence of the Islamic testimony of faith in which there is no reality but the one Reality and no god but the one God. The actualization of this choice gradually brings about the perfection and ultimately the transcendence of the human being, this being the challenge amounting to a sacred vocation in the pursuit of life and the goal of the human entity.

No one has ever suggested that being human is easy; but through the force of free will, human beings have the possibility of manifesting themselves fully in this life with a view to perfecting themselves in the next life. This possibility runs through us as a direct blessing from God through the faculty of the will in which we can anticipate the consequences of our actions. By choosing the path of the good and the true, a person can participate in the beatitude of the Divine Being according to their individual nature and destiny.

Through the intelligence, we contain the essence of a knowledge of the totality; but a knowledge of the One is not enough to traverse the pathways of this life. Through the will, we can bring that knowledge and that truth down into the very fabric of our being to the extent that the texture of truth becomes interwoven within us as a single and fully integrated reality. Intelligence contains the essential knowledge of the Divinity, but through desire, free will makes the union with God a genuine possibility and a living experience.

♣ ♣ ♣

As an existential reality and in principle, the human being is an open door to a transcendent reality. The spiritual instincts and a heightened spiritual imagination have taught us that much about ourselves. Our free will can close the door to the Infinite, however, and we can begin our journey through this life via another entrance if we so choose.

The dilemma facing people today is as existential and real as it is perennial and fraught with consequences. The truth is that there is a fundamental ambiguity at the heart of the human condition that keeps us guessing and clouds the true object of our desire. It is the ambiguity of this true objective that draws us into the darkening shadows of our mind even though the emerging light is there to behold in the firmament of our mind. It is the perennial doubt concerning the true nature of reality that leads people to believe in the evidence of the finite world they can physically sense rather than the infinite world of the spirit. It is the uncertainty implicit in the cosmic veil that separates human beings from the direct knowledge of God and only permits them glimpses of the Eternal to the extent that they make efforts to lift the veil that separates them from the truth; it is the freedom to deny the premise and the promise of another world after death and to affirm the illusions and the sensory appeal of this world instead. It is the temptation to seek the fulfillment of one's desires in the promise of an immediate satisfaction within the realm of the tangible and the visible rather than in the enduring vision of union with the Supreme Being.

The perennial ambiguity of life finds its resolution through an infinite number of choices during the course of a life, choices that in truth reflect only one inescapable choice: It goes by many names, including the Transcendent, the Eternal, the Infinite, the Absolute, the Sovereign Good, and the Supreme Intelligence, but ultimately represents the one and only Reality. Every single moment contains the essence of this choice, while alternatively every act of free will contains a movement, a direction, and a consequence that should be considered before people choose what they want and moves headlong into their future.

Needless to say, the freely choosing human being is compelled to exercise free choice. Alas, the paradox returns to haunt us. If people make a choice that leads in the direction of disequilibrium and disharmony—conditions that are difficult to deny since they are everywhere apparent—they must bear this in mind as a consequence of their choice and invite the misery and unhappiness that must inevitably accompany the wrong desire. The force of the will can also recreate a sense of balance and equilibrium through the right desire. Every thought, every decision, and every choice paves the way for a change in the perception of the self, while the will represents the faculty of measure and balance, of forward direction and of arrival at a state of equilibrium in this world as a prelude to the transformation of the soul in the next world.

We do not want to regret in retrospect what we should have become by virtue of the nature of the human condition. It is a condition of life that we live in accordance with the dictates of our given nature as human beings within the context of a genuine understanding of the true nature of reality. At stake here is the knowledge of who we are and what our place and role is in the design of the universe. That is why it is virtually a mandate of the human condition that people need to take a stand concerning what they believe in, for they must give an accounting of what they have accomplished in their life. That is why the vast resources of the entire scientific community have set themselves the goal of identifying the true nature of reality and seek to develop a theory of everything that will describe that reality. That is why we have free will and the concomitant power of free choice, because in choosing what we think and what we believe, and what we actually accomplish, we are creating and recreating ourselves anew at every moment in time, a participation of self that anticipates the timeless moment within every moment through the light of the mind and the empowering force of the will.

Essentially, knowledge of the truth obliges a person to choose the truth. As different as the great world religions are in their formal aspect, they all agree on the need for us to live our life wisely and well. This may not come easy and mistakes will happen; at some point, every person must trip and fall, only to pick themselves up again and continue on their way with the knowledge of the truth to guide their footsteps forward. To live life wisely is to live in accordance with the knowledge of God, Who sets the parameters for the reality we experience in this world. To live life well is to forsake one's weaknesses and limitations, to choose the good and reject the alternative of evil, to make every effort to perfect oneself in this life, and ultimately to transcend the individual world of the self for the liberating dimensions of the Higher Self. "The purpose of freedom is to enable us to choose what we are in the depths of our heart."[6]

In order to *choose* what we are, however, we must *know* what we are. That is why free will implies intelligence above all—an intelligence that contains the ability to act upon that which we know to be true about ourselves and the world. Can post-modern society assert the privilege of freedom without the individuals of that society understanding their true inner nature and the limitations that accompany the reality of their existence? The problem of freedom does not necessarily lie in its definition of terms; the dilemma of the will as free does not lie in its qualifying freedom. The dark power of free will lies within the modern sensibility and finds its underlying roots in its conception of self. No matter how deep the secular, scientific establishment digs into the atomic realms of the body, no matter how far down it explores into the nether regions of the unconscious, no matter how persistently it attempts to reduce the human image as a shadow-image and reflection of God into the elementary particles of the subatomic world, no matter how long it searches for the ultimate description of life and the final proof of humanity's true reality, the scientific worldview of today will never arrive at a convincing portrait of the human self image. It will never fully appreciate the knowledge of the human revelation that enjoys in principle a luminous intelligence and mediating will and that serves as a link between the two natures of good and evil and as a bridge between the concomitant worlds of Heaven and Earth.

6. Frithjof Schuon, *To Have a Center* (Bloomington, IN: World Wisdom Books, 1990), p. 38.

Chapter Nine

♣

Weaving the Loom of Language

The universe is a great man and man is a little universe.
  (Sufi saying)

Man has been truly termed a 'microcosm,' or little world in himself, and
the structure of his body should be studied not only by those who wish to
become doctors, but by those who wish to attain to a more intimate knowledge of God.
  (Al-Ghazali)

The probing account of a sacred science of mind has revealed an
unfinished being that does not know its true self and has not fully rec-
onciled its relationship with the world. It is a mind in search of a quintessential knowledge that could resolve all inner doubt about the true
nature of reality, and a mind in search of a quintessential form of
behavior that could bring about its transfiguration, a potential that lies
secreted within the human being as a promise awaiting fulfillment. It
is a quest for meaning and certitude that leads from the kind of being
that we know we are not and never were, such as the anthropoid and
the ape, to the kind of being that we are in principle and hope to
become, such as the "primordial man," the "true man," and the "perfect man" of the traditional world religions. It is a central quest that
takes place within the distinctive domain of the human kingdom
rather than the broad expanse of the animal kingdom, a quest that
partakes of a curious inner light of unknown origin that permits us to
achieve our fullest potential during the course of life, to become something that no animal has ever been before or ever will be.

The narrative account of the human passage through time and
mythic tale of deliverance takes place primarily within the inner
world, contrary perhaps to the vivid and definitive experience of the
physical, sensory, and phenomenal world of nature that serves as the
external and natural habitat. It is an intuitive, emotional, and imaginal world that is fraught with sinister danger because we are *Homo
duplex*, a creature composed of body and spirit and thus a being that

167

manifests a split image of the self. We unevenly embody the elements of animal and saint, while our soul comprises impulses of both darkness and light. Because of the distinctive and pivotal nature of the human faculties and the condition of the inner cosmos that forms the framework of our active consciousness, our spirit is able to walk readily from one world to the other without formally observing and being bothered by any of the boundaries that we pass in the process. As we have suggested in earlier chapters of this work, because of the full range of our faculties and because of the nature of the borderland they inhabit, we are equally at home in the phenomenal world as we are in the world of the spirit, at least in principle.

To negotiate our way through the vicissitudes of life, we enjoy a number of inner faculties that entitle us to the name that not only distinguishes us from earlier forms within the genus *Homo* but that has been adopted to characterize us during the historical era when the species *Homo sapiens* emerged as a distinctive category within the genus *Homo*.[1] The human kingdom that we were destined to enter and fully inhabit came into existence and is characterized by the truly human faculties that make us what we are, not *Homo erectus* or *Homo habilis*, but *Homo sapiens*:[2] a wise human being whose intelligence is a light, whose consciousness is a mirror, whose imagination is a field, whose higher emotion is a flame, and whose virtue is a perfume, at least according to traditional symbolism.

The human kingdom that the primordial Adam and Eve entered and took possession of did not happen through the back door of a physical evolution so meticulously described by modern scientists, but through the creative and intelligent design of a Creator who has made possible the direct descent of the first generation man and woman, not through what some scientists have called

1. Technically speaking, humans are classified by scientists in the mammalian order of Primates. Within this order, humans are placed alongside what are identified as "our nearest living relative," the apes in the family of Hominidae. The separate human line in the hominid family is distinguished by being placed in a sub-family, Homininae, whose members are then called hominines. It would all sound rather depressing, if not disquieting, if it were not for the fact that these speculations are actually modern-day figments of the purely secular imagination.
2. Not everyone of course holds this view. John Gribbin, in his book *In Search of the Double Helix* (Baltimore, Md: Penguin, 1995), suggests that we put our "prejudices" aside by placing humanity, *Homo*, into a separate category on the evolutionary branch, to be called *Pan sapiens*, referring to a small still-living ape called *Pan paniscus*.

the "rapid branching"[3] of a discontinuous process of evolution from primate to ape to hominid to *Homo erectus*, but rather as a human creation in principle and as such. Although the primordial human archetype contained the seeds of becoming a revelatory oracle of mystery as well as an implicit promise of fulfillment and enlightenment, in this fallen condition as earthly wayfarers and seekers after truth, the earthly prototype in its historical manifestation is still an incomplete, unfinished being. This idea is later echoed in one of the essays of Emerson when he says that "the man is only half himself, the other half is his expression."[4]

Unlike the instinctive world of the animal kingdom, *Homo sapiens* displays an otherness in the human kingdom amounting to a singularity of soul and a uniqueness of being that no other animal comes remotely near to approximating. Certain animals may approach this kingdom and look within, such as the chimps and the apes with their physical analogies and their corporeal proximity of shape and stance, but none of them have taken leave of their given domain, crossed the narrow bridge over the bottomless chasm of species (speciation), and passed through the invisible door of consciousness into the world of humanity. Indeed, even common sense suggests that they will never bid farewell to their rightful provenance. Instead of suggesting, by way of analogy or through molecular composition, their proximity to humankind and their link in the shadows of its evolution, the apes and hominids serve as poignant reminders of what humankind is not. They have all remained at the edge of the antediluvian forest as silent sentinels of the essentially closed and magical world of humankind.

Humanity makes a noble animal of the human race, but noble animals will never exhibit the humanity that is the summative and prevailing characteristic of the human race. The great horned stag, the majestic eagle, and the graceful swan not only display nobility through their physical presence, but actually highlight their meaning and thus express a particular aspect of the Divinity, in profile as

3. On the transitional steps between the primates and humanity, Phillip Johnson writes in his compelling critique of Darwinism: "We have to imagine what Steven Stanley calls 'rapid branching,' a euphemism for mysterious leaps, which somehow produced the human mind and spirit from animal materials" (*Darwin on Trial* [Downers Grove, Ill: InterVarsity Press, 2nd ed., 1993], p. 86).
4. Ralph Waldo Emerson, *Essays*, p. 13.

it were; yet nothing about these animals, or any others, suggests a possible transcendence of their individual form or implies some kind of escape from their given nature through their own capacity or effort. The owl reminds us of the virtue of wisdom, but the owl is not wise. Like the ape that remains forever at the edge of the forest, animals represent particular aspects of the Divinity, but they will never take leave of their given form and will never depart from the kingdom of their animal nature. No matter how high an individual animal intelligence may reach—and some animals are very intelligent indeed—their private world remains locked within that individual destiny and will never take leave of their given station. That is why animals are called horizontal in the possibilities of their projection, while humans are referred to as vertical beings, capable of transcendending all that takes place within the animal kingdom and which makes of us the *mirandum Dei opus*, or the masterpiece of God.

According to the traditional worldview, being human qualifies us for certain entitlements, not the least being that we can leave behind the limited confines of the instinctive world of animals in order to participate in the broad canvas of the human kingdom; but that is not enough. The Scholastics used to say: "*Homo non proprie humanus sed superhumanus est*"—which means that to be properly human, a person must go beyond being merely human. The kind of instinctive knowledge and the vital, and in some instances, noble actions displayed by animals are not enough to define humanity. We display the significance and meaning of our humanity through our intuitive intelligence, powers of abstract reasoning, moral sensibility, quixotic imagination, unique personality, and the complex realm of our moral, ethical, and spiritual aspirations. Still, this is not enough.

We have a mind that reacts to the stimulus of knowledge, a reason that analyzes cognitive thinking and follows the clear line of logic, a consciousness that brings a heightened awareness to every thought and action, an imagination that envisions alternative worlds and reacts to the impulses of the soul, and a heart that denotes the inner pulse of our moral being. Still, this is not enough to qualify as the Taoist "true man" or the Islamic "perfect man," a living image of the Divinity and a hieroglyphic symbol of an enigmatic creature whose inner message contains a mystery that needs to be understood on its own rather than human terms. In order to explain the most fundamental of all the discontinuities in nature, we need something more than the "prebiotic soup" theory[5] of origins and the corporeal and cranial resemblances—dissemblance may be a more appropriate word—to the representatives of the simian kingdom, to account for all that *Homo sapiens* finds within itself and in its relationship with the universe.

The decisive factors within the human kingdom and the inner cosmos of which we write are the discernment of the Real from the illusory and ultimately the union of the human being with that Reality. That is why human beings have inner faculties that will lead them through this wilderness and ultimately guide them across the borders of the mind and the horizon of the self. Human beings must express the knowledge that they attain as internalized wisdom and must exhibit their behavior and actions as consummate virtues. In order to transcend the individual self for union with the Greater Self, we must transcend the limitations of our individual nature and go beyond the needs and desires of the individual self. We need to know *a priori* the source of our origins, the meaning of our life and the true nature of our final end toward which all human effort is projected and against which all the wealth of this world is as nothing. To that end, we have a number of higher faculties that make our "little universe" a true reflection of the "great man" that is the macro-universe.

♣ ♣ ♣

One thing that we have perhaps forgotten during the modern era, in the rush to construct a grand architecture of an empirical and neutral science with the aid of the rational mind and the brutal assessment of our senses, is the significance of wisdom as the culmination of the human condition. We no longer live within the light of an ageless and traditional knowledge that has the capacity to become internalized as a fully realized wisdom. In a sense, the very concept of wisdom has become a kind of museum piece, an

5. "'Warm little pond' was how Darwin described the prebiotic environment in which 'life' might have originated from inanimate matter in an 1871 letter to a friend" (*The Creation Hypothesis: Scientific Evidence for an Intelligent Designer*, ed. J. P. Mooreland [Downers Grove, Ill: Intervarsity Press, 1994], p. 175).

artifact of humanity and of history, periodically held up to the light, then returned to its pedestal and safely preserved under protective glass to be remembered as the *sophia* from days of yore. In the value system we now emulate, people need to be rational, sensible, and practical, but not necessarily wise.

In today's climate of opinion, we behave as if we have fully accepted and absorbed the quintessential mystery of origins that modern science has resolved and imposed upon us as the basis of the modern paradigm of knowledge concerning the origin of life and the universe. Yet, the lure of the Absolute and the Real continues to haunt our psyche, our imagination, and our souls in spite of the modern denial of the inner self and the reckless affirmation of the world. We are fascinated with the power that scientific and technical knowledge brings, but we will not be saved either by the weight of its pretensions or from the gravity and entropy of a world without wisdom.

Another thing we have forgotten is the importance of wisdom as a frame of reference during the course of a life. It is one of the key spiritual prerogatives that guide the course of human events. During these times, wisdom has become notable by virtue of its absence; and yet there was a more traditional time when wisdom made its presence felt through its unique power to shape a person's judgment and affect their behavior. Wisdom manifests itself as a distinctive influence within the human kingdom through three separate modes of expression, most notably through revelation, nature, and the human soul.

The correspondence between revelation, the natural order, and the human soul is crucial in the spiritual configuration of every religious tradition, partly because each of these factors forms an essential part of the source material of the religion and partly because the written wisdom, the natural wisdom, and the human wisdom contained in scripture, nature, and the human soul all deliver the essential knowledge that bespeaks the true nature of the one Reality. As such, revelation, nature and the soul each represent signposts that are direct vehicles of the knowledge of God; as such, they are intended to serve humankind as a means of lifting the veil that separates people from the direct knowledge of the Divinity.

Wisdom begins as a formal descent of knowledge through the words and verses of sacred scripture. These verses become the signs and symbols that are woven into the fabric of the natural order to become part of the rhythms of the universe. According to the traditionalist French writer René Guénon, "the whole of nature amounts to no more than a symbol of the transcendent realities."[6] In a sense, everything in the manifested world exists as a symbol of a higher knowledge to the extent that not only the scriptures, but also nature and the human soul are considered symbolic forms of revelation and vital sources of knowledge, serving as an opening onto the world of the transcendent reality. "Wisdom is to perceive the symbolism of things."[7] There is an implicit wisdom embedded within the forms of the universe that serves as a reminder of the origin and source of a transforming knowledge that actually amounts to an argument on behalf of an Intelligent Designer by virtue of the implicit order, design, and wisdom woven into the very structure of the natural order and become part of the rhythms of the universe. Ralph Waldo Emerson summarizes this idea simply and succinctly: "The Supreme Being does not build up nature around us, but puts it forth through us."[8]

The argument for a wise designer and supreme intelligence responsible for the creation of the universe dominated the traditional worldview of previous ages. Traditional humanity sustained a belief in this worldview partly because it sounded inherently plausible and partly because it satisfied common sense, unlike the modern theory of evolution which may appeal to the human desire to be free of ethical responsibility and moral choice, but curiously fails on a number of levels to satisfy the dictates of common sense in suggesting that chance mutations and random design could have haphazardly thrown together so many things of such complexity and ingenuity on the order of an entire universe with a myriad of living organisms and arrive at such perfections of design and utility as the human eye or a bird's feather. The existence of an implicit wisdom written into the fabric of the human being and into the rhythms of nature contains ample explanatory

6. René Guénon, *The Symbolism of the Cross*, trans. Angus Macnab (London: Luzac, 1975), p. 14.
7. Frithjof Schuon, *Roots of the Human Condition* (Bloomington, IN: World Wisdom Books, 1991), p. 57.
8. *Ralph Waldo Emerson*, ed. Richard Poirier (Oxford: Oxford University Press, 1990), p. 30.

power to sufficiently resolve the universal mystery of the creation in favor of a God who created it.

The classical argument for Divinity recognized the pattern and design of the natural order and understood that the specified complexity of living organisms could not have arisen by purely natural and random causes but instead required an intelligent first Cause. Isaac Newton expressed a common sentiment of his time when he declared: "This most beautiful system of the sun, planets, and comets, could only proceed from the counsel and dominion of an intelligent and powerful Being."[9] In keeping with this principle of analogy between belief in the argument for first origins from design and the evidence based on observational premises of the implicit order discovered in nature, people of former times comprehended at face value and willingly believed in the knowing wisdom of a Supreme Being, which Islam identifies through the names the All-Knowing (*al-Alim*) and the Wise (*al-Hakim*).

For the traditional mentality, wisdom lies embedded within the very shapes and forms of the universe. It shines through the colors of the rainbow that reaches down with its shimmering image of color and light to touch the earth in blessing before disappearing once again into the mist. It recalls the perfection within the design of snow crystals and the calm within the eye of the storm. It summons the beauty encompassed within the artistic pattern of a butterfly wing and the message of order and design behind the spider's web. The elaboration of the seasons, the miracle of color, sight, and sound, the diversity of the animal kingdom, the harmonious motion of the planets, and the magisterial procession of the intergalactic bodies all suggest an intelligence and a wisdom that must transcend anything random, fortuitous, or merely human. Indeed, the entire fabric of the natural order, with its intricate design and seemingly harmonious interconnectedness, captures within its structures and forms the incredible wisdom of the Divinity and places the mind and senses at the heart of it all as the observer and listener in search of a knowledge and in pursuit of a virtue that is theirs to behold and experience.

Scientists today go to great lengths to associate the perennial mysteries of mind, intelligence, use of language, and sense of con-

---

9. Isaac Newton, "General Schohum," in *Mathematical Principles of Natural Philosophy*, quoted in *Great Books of the Western World* (Chicago, 1952), p. 360.

sciousness with purely natural phenomena.[10] These are the aspects of humanity that represent the final frontier of mystery that have yet to surrender their secrets and may never do so. Yet scientists refuse to affirm the distinctive intelligence directly reflected in the wisdom of the human body and the cognitive intelligence associated with the abstract manipulation of language. With the discovery of the genetic code and the elucidation of the structure of DNA, modern scientists breathed a collective sigh of relief when it was shown that there was an incredible similarity of the human genetic makeup with the simian world of monkeys and apes. Indeed the existence of the genetic code seemed to lend great credence to the theory of a common ancestor.[11] Unfortunately, the discovery has settled nothing concerning human origins and has raised more questions than it has answered, for scientists have no idea as to the origin of the genetic code, how it functions, and what its implicit wisdom actually means in terms of origin theory. They have not successfully articulated a definitive refutation of the concept of a supreme intelligence as First Cause beyond flatly refusing to consider it as a theoretical option.

On the contrary, if ever proof was needed to identify a specific phenomenon of the natural order that traces a divine origin by displaying an innate intelligence and a wisdom packed together as a comprehensive information system that processes energy and makes a living structure possible, the discovery of the existence of the genetic code is that proof. The base sequences of DNA virtually spell out in coded form the instructions that allow a cell to make the proteins that ultimately form every aspect of the human body. The genetic code, understood as the genetic letters in the book of humanity that actually comprises an encyclopedia of information, is a molecular communication system in the form of a symbolic code that functions in the same way that the letters of the alphabet

10. Darwin sounded the death knell for the argument for an intelligent and wise Being when he suggested that natural selection produced an "apparent design," thereby putting to rest once and for all any suggestion of a superior intelligence or first cause behind the design of the natural order.
11. Tests at the molecular level have shown that human, chimpanzee, and gorilla DNA are identical along at least 98 percent of their length. The "unique" features of humanity are contained in less than 2 percent of our DNA. John Gribbin concludes that "people are, in a very real sense, infant apes" (*In Search of the Double Helix*, p. 343).

function, namely as a system of symbols to communicate information and convey meaning. We call this knowledge contained within the genetic code wisdom because like all true wisdom, it not only exists in principle as knowledge, but also acts upon that knowledge to make something miraculous like the human body.

Now, no one in their right mind would contest the fact that an intelligent communication in words presupposes an intelligent mind to articulate such a communication. Through the principle of analogy, it is not unreasonable to conclude that the incredible message sequences embedded within the genetic code of DNA suggest the presence of an intelligent, indeed a supra-natural source. From the scientific point of view, there is no convincing, experimental evidence to indicate how this has come about and what drives it to work to such perfection, at least not empirical evidence from natural causes. In fact, the only real evidence we have to date is that it does take not only intelligence but a profound wisdom to produce the high level information sequencing that takes place within the ascending ladder of the genetic code in creating what amounts to the wisdom of the body.

♣ ♣ ♣

That the curious mind can ask a question at all and then attempt to answer it leads us to highlight one final attribute that definitely separates human beings from all other living creatures and places them well within the rarefied environment of the human kingdom. We refer of course to the use of human language to weave the fabric of our minds into a form of speech that can be communicated to others and understood by everyone. In his discourse entitled *Cratylus*, Plato refers to the "loom of language" while Cicero, in a work entitled *De natura deorum*, observed that words are "the notes of things" (*vocabula sunt notae rerum*). Lucretius had the following observation to make concerning human language: "as for the various sounds of spoken language, it was nature that drove men to utter these, and practical convenience that gave the form to the names of objects" (V, 1928ff).[12]

12. Lucretius, quoted in Kathleen Gibson, *The Loom of Language* (Cambridge: Cambridge University Press, 1995), p. 21.

In the traditional view, language is not a survival advantage resulting from a process within the natural order or a "practice convenience" amounting to no more than "notes" on some scale of communication; on the contrary, it serves as the singular mode of communication of a conscious and reflective being whose unique faculties come together and act in unison through the synthesizing quality of the intelligence and the practical ability of the vocal cords to give voice to both thoughts and desires.[13] We speak our mind and by doing so are able to draw upon a language of the self that makes our intelligence not only audible but actually physical, uniting what we know with what we are able to put into spoken words or written form in order to communicate to the world.

Throughout the millennia, the gift of speech has always been one of the hallmarks of the traditional perspective, which distinguished human beings from the animals and underscored the very essence and meaning of their humanity. According to the Quran, Adam was taught "the names of things" (2:31) while the Bible says that "whatever Adam called every living creature, that was the name thereof" (Genesis 2:19). This knowledge distinguished him from both the angels and the animals because of the unique power he enjoyed to articulate, through sound symbols, the "names of things" in the form of a language that permitted him to communicate his innermost thoughts and convey their meaning. He could consciously think, know, and give voice through the gift of words to a complete and natural language system that could reason through abstract thoughts, communicate an infinite range of speculative ideas, and describe the world around him. This ability represented tremendous power and incredible prescience of mind; it was tantamount to permitting not only Adam but all future generations to think about and articulate in words their own meaning of the world.

Perhaps our intuition, intelligence, consciousness, and higher emotions highlight the essential characteristics of our humanity; yet it is language that makes us feel human. Our inner world of

---

13. For some, there is no question concerning the origin of human language, although many reasonable people might wonder why this is so. "That spoken human language *did* emerge from the melting pot of hominid evolution is unquestionable. But, because of its nature, *why* or *when* it arose must remain forever the secret of times past" (Richard Leakey, *People of the Lake: Mankind and its Beginnings* [New York: Avon Books, 1978], p. 171) (italics mine).

imaginative thinking and the continuous inner dialogue with our conscience all become known to the outside world through words. The spoken and written word creates images, tells stories, and stirs emotions. Through language, we can articulate the sense of our own identity and make ourselves known to the world. Thomas Henry Huxley, the well-known friend and champion of Darwin, wrote in 1863: "No one is more strongly convinced than I am of the vastness of the gulf between . . . man and the brutes . . . for he alone possesses the marvelous endowment of intelligible and rational speech [and] . . . stands raised upon it as on a mountaintop, far above the level of his humble fellows."[14]

When Adam was given the names of things, he actually took possession of the world and became, as the Quran relates, the *khalifat Allah*, or God's representative on earth. By way of compensation, he discovered the unique dimension of the self, a world within a world that left the world of primal utterances and primitive emotive cries behind and opened up the vista of a higher consciousness and a higher form of expression never before witnessed outside the human kingdom. This represented a primordial human condition that distinguished humans from the rest of the creation and was the mental counterpart to the symbolic vertical stance represented on the physical plane of being. It represented an external sign of an inner process that went so far beyond the physical senses that the higher mind could speculate about the farthest reaches of the universe and look beyond its physical being into the past and future of itself. Through vibration, sound, rhythm, intonation, and ultimately through prayer and worship, the higher mind and heart could utter the deepest secrets of their inmost yearning. The mystery of intelligent thought and the act of the spoken and written word combined to create for humanity a language of self that would not only prove the intelligence in measurable form, but also reveal the inmost thoughts concerning the mystery of the highest reality.

Not everyone, however, holds this view of language and its origins. In fact, next to the perennial debate concerning the origin of the universe and of life itself by intelligent design or by natural causes, perhaps nothing has become as contentious as the gift of

14. T. H. Huxley, quoted in Richard Leakey, *Origins Reconsidered: In Search of What Makes Us Human*, p. 240.

language:[15] how it originated, how it is learned, how it functions with reference to natural processes of the body and how it is rationalized into a meaningful system of communication. Is language a unique human characteristic or is it merely the extension and enhancement of cognitive capacities whose inception and ultimate source may be found among the grunts and murmurs of apes or the echolocation of dolphins, bats, and whales?

In the 1874 revised version of *The Descent of Man*, Darwin wrote: "I cannot doubt that language owes its origin to the imitation and modification of various natural sounds, the voices of other animals, and man's own instinctive cries."[16] Such a suggestion may seem incredible today, given the level of human achievement in the realms of art, literature, science, and technology; but dealing with these incredible abilities, not to mention the very nature of the bodily form, has given rise for over a hundred years to the conundrum associating the mystery and miracle of the human being with the mindless (yet disturbingly creative) processes of natural selection and the analogous similarities humanity shares with the animal kingdom. For example, Darwin asks if "some wise ape-like animal" might not "have imitated the growl of a beast of prey and thus told his fellow-monkeys the nature of the expected danger?" Then, in the next clause, he suggests, "this would have been a first step in the formation of a language."[17] One can only speculate if Darwin was just trying to accommodate a difficult question on the periphery of his developing theory, or whether he actually believed that only a short step led beyond the communication system of a chimp or a gorilla into the world of the human language system and the vast cognitive complexity, the abstract reasoning, and the creative heights that it entails.

Fortunately, idle speculation concerning the true nature of human language and its implications has evolved since the time of Darwin. In recent times, vast resources and enormous amounts of money have been invested in an attempt to teach chimps and gorillas the use of language in a manner that might approximate

15. We refer here to language generally, although there exist over 5,000 languages globally to actually accomplish the job that language in principle was created to accomplish.
16. Charles Darwin, *The Descent of Man* (New York: D. Appleton, 1874), p. 87.
17. *The Creation Hypothesis*, ed. J. P. Mooreland, p. 236.

human usage, presumably to lend further evidence in support of the theory of the close proximity of humans with their simian ancestors through such a direct link as the evolution of language from primate to hominid to present-day men and women. One can only wonder what other purpose could be involved here, except perhaps the interest of the truth, to somehow justify such research on a higher philosophical level. For example, what would it mean for us to finally prove that these animals could be taught to communicate and use language in the same manner as their human cousins? Would we have to surrender our position as God's unique thinking creation and adapt to the reality of our talking cousins? Would our intelligence somehow be compromised in associating the miracle of language with nothing more than the capacity of a chimp to articulate its desires and ask for the moon? One can only speculate about the desired outcome of such speculative research rather than anticipating the awful consequences of such a fact.

The issue of whether animals can be made to talk can only be mentioned here in passing as a point of interest and can certainty not be resolved. It has turned into yet another lengthy battle surrounding the theory of evolution and its place in the philosophical worldview of modern civilization. Yet, it is worth mentioning that the results achieved to date, although remarkable in their individual efforts and outcomes, do not justify the hyperbolic claims[18] that the animals studied and trained could approximate the language spoken by humans. Even infant children, who through a perfectly natural process far removed from the rigorous training that the chimps receive, are able to acquire and command the use of all the basic grammar and structures of the language.

Perhaps the most revealing aspect of the research to date highlights what the chimps and gorillas cannot do. For one thing, the apes are universally incapable of entering into any abstract thought and make common everyday associations in keeping with the linguistic ability of ordinary human children. They can only use the sign symbols and handle the immediate situation to which they had

---

18. The distinguished Harvard professor emeritus D. L .Bolinger once wrote that a couple of well-known chimpanzees had "matched the language ability of a four-year-old child and . . . proved that creatures other than humans had the intelligence to transfer meaning and to create syntax" (*Aspects of Language* [New York: Harcourt Brace Jovanovich, 1975], p. 29).

been trained to respond within a very specific context. Thus, their linguistic ability was found wanting and they were not able to apply what they had learned for other hypothetical abstractions. According to Thomas Sebeok: "That apes can be taught fairly large vocabularies of symbols has been well established. Time and again, however, reports indicate that there is only a faint resemblance between a chimpanzee's or a gorilla's application of these newly acquired tools and that of humans."[19]

Moreover, the apes displayed a complete inability to use syntactical structures of grammar, which represent the supporting skeletal bones of all languages that all normal children quickly learn and rely upon. The correct syntactical meaning between the phrase "the dog chased the car" and "the car chased the dog" would immediately be apprehended by any child. In the phrase "time eat," the chimp is trained to respond to the phrase to indicate that it is time to eat; and yet there is no way of knowing or proving that the chimp actually knows or appreciates the concept of time beyond responding to the impulse of hunger and the perceived desire to eat *at that time,* and not that it wants to eat because it is the appropriate time.

The respected linguist Noam Chomsky calls this aspect of language usage the "structure-dependence" principle. Children, as a matter of course, make distinctions between many grammatical categories including sentence structure as well as the role of words within the sentence, such as subject, verb, and object. The chimps can produce chained responses that they had learned by rote repetition through association and reward, but they cannot make distinctions of meaning resulting from the structures of grammar, which are embedded within the syntax of all sentences.

This leads to another, peripheral point worth mentioning: Children learn language naturally in a communicative and functionally interactive setting through listening, association, and response. They hear, listen, observe, mimic, imitate, and eventually begin to speak in the natural setting of their homes, without much effort and as a matter of course. By the time they begin their schooling, they are already adepts in the understanding and usage of all the fundamental structures of the language. Whatever the chimps

19. Thomas A. Sebeok and Jean Umiker-Sebeok, eds., *Speaking of Apes: A Critical Anthology of Two-Way Communication with Man* (New York: Plenum, 1981), p. 272.

and apes have managed to learn, on the other hand, has been the result of a systematic and intensive effort of devoted and sophisticated researchers to instill a few hundred sign symbols that have been tirelessly drilled into them through repetition and satisfaction reinforcement. This is not exactly the setting of natural selection and survival of the fittest, free of all intelligent design and purpose, that evolutionary experts prefer to rely on for their explanations into the patterns of evolutionary development.

Perhaps the most revealing—and symbolic—limitation of the language-learning behavior of the apes is the fact that they do not ask questions. Beyond the inevitably complicated syntactical structures required of questions, not to mention the time factor, they simply do not seem to understand what a question is. It is as if making an inquiry is quite simply too far beyond their means, in spite of the fact that they are notoriously well known for being inquisitive animals. The telling interrogative why never became part of their repertoire and remains to this day clearly beyond their cognitive reach. Even a young child, on the other hand, distinguishes itself through the perennial nature of its inquiries, making possible the very pursuit of a knowledge that has brought us from the edge of the primeval forest to the very edge of the universe.

The underlying presumption of the research into the language-learning capacity of certain animals would certainty tend to debunk the traditional belief that the symbolic force of the human ability to communicate through language makes us unique beings among the creation and separates us from the rest of the animal kingdom in a manner that will never be trespassed. A modern-day assumption seems to be that if a direct link can be established between the language ability of animals and humanity and that if the only thing effectively stopping the apes from actually speaking comes from the inherent limitations of their vocal cords and not from any deficiency of their native intelligence, then a very strong case could be established to lend support to the common ancestor theory of evolution. To date, however, the gulf that exists between animal and human intelligence is inviolate and the proof is in the inability of animals to learn to approximate any form of truly human language as all humans know and experience it, namely abstract reasoning, cognitive thinking, and the creative flow of language that make sophisticated forms of communication at all possible.

♣ ♣ ♣

The linguistic chasm between the animal and human kingdoms echoes, in a curious way, the great divide that exists between inanimate matter and living organisms. In the pursuit of the grand inquiry into a natural and empirically scientific explanation with the capacity to prove beyond a reasonable doubt the basic mysteries of the universe, the rational mind arrives at a moment and place in time when cognitive thinking, on its own, reaches the end of the road. The place represents a chasm which cannot be crossed, which defines the duality of the world, and the moment represents the instant when rational thinking ends along with the pursuit of science, the moment when the finitude of time as expressed by Einstein, Hawking, and Penrose finally terminates in order to make way for an act of creation that is independent of the space-time dimension, a "divine singularity" if you will, to complement and bring to fruition the "initial singularity" of modern science.

The amazing thing about this chasm is that human beings are able to cross it in spite of the limitations of the rational mind and the knowledge gathered by the efforts of modern scientific inquiry. The broad gulf that separates mind from matter and that divides inanimate matter from living organisms can only be crossed through the intervention of a Supreme Intelligence and the premeditation of a Wise Designer. What we have attempted to portray by reflecting upon the inner cosmos of the mind during the course of this work is that we are much more than our mind alone. The human kingdom is virtually defined by the solitary image that the primordial Adam casts in cameo of the Transcendent Intelligence and as an earthly shadow of the Divine Light. In addition to the phenomenal world of nature and the sensory experience of that world, we draw upon the reflections and insights of an inner world in which we move as in a borderland that both separates and unites the life of the world and the life of the spirit.

Language has been irrevocably linked and gives voice to the inner faculties and higher power of the mind, as the various spiritual traditions have always maintained. It is not the natural evolution of the grunts and groans of primates, nor the primal cries and warning calls of animals in the wild that have given rise to the articulation of abstract thought, much less the great vocal skills of humans such as the talent of debating and the power of oration.

Everything in nature, both animate and inanimate, emits sound of one kind or another—even a drop falling on water adds its note to the sonant symphony of the natural environment. Birds sing, but the song of the nightingale and the song of a human voice highlight, not the language acquisition capabilities of animals and humans over eons of time, but rather the vast distance that exists between the two species in terms of both vocal ability and the mental power that vocal ability represents.

The use of language is the final, external destination of the inner faculties of mind. As the ultimate defining power, language actually puts the seal on the entire range of the faculties within the inner human cosmos. Through the symbolic use of words, we can describe our inner world and create a captivating narrative of our feelings and emotions, thereby bringing to a sublime conclusion what began as a subtle intuition to take leave of the limited self. With language, we can articulate all the axioms of mathematics and ultimately invest with meaning all the thought processes that relate forms of language to the sensory impressions that are grounded in the world of sensorial experience, namely the world of science.

Through an astute manipulation of words, we can create grand works of philosophy, literature, theatre, and indeed science. Through words, we echo the Word of God uttered at the initial moment of creation[20] and revisited through every revealed word of scripture, and we worship and praise the Divinity through prayer and invocation. Nor is language the mere use of speech or the written word; it assumes a multitude of forms including verbal thought, the gestures and body language that convey meaning, and the symbolic sign language used by the deaf, in addition to the language of the genetic code that actually builds the message of the human body within the very cells of our being.

We began this work by reflecting upon the source of human intelligence; we will end by commenting on its consequences. A profoundly complementary relationship exists between the use of

---

20. In the Christian tradition, the *Logos* became man. The "Word of God" is personified and identified in the person of Jesus. John writes in the Gospel: "In the beginning was the Word, and the Word was with God, and the Word was God" (John 1:1). According to the Quran, God uttered the primordial sound *Kun*, meaning "be," and the universe came into existence and *became* a reality, while the Quran itself—like Christ—is the supreme *Logos*, the direct "Word" of God.

language and the human intelligence that makes the spoken word possible. Human language reflects the entire range of the human faculties and actually makes their content known to the world. Through the higher faculty of the intellect, we receive a direct transmission from above and are able to absorb the essential knowledge of God without any barrier or veil. We apprehend the truth with certainty through the intellect, but it is with language that we proclaim this truth, witness our faith, and worship the Divinity. Through the imagination, heart, emotions and higher sentiments, we can perceive a world that reaches beyond our immediate senses; but only through language can we describe and put into words this inner world with a high degree of precision and accuracy, and only through presence of mind, reflection, and creativity can we communicate the substance of our minds to others. Through the powers of mind and the luminous source of our intelligence, we can negotiate our way through the life of this world; but we can also go beyond the border of the time-space dimension to envision the vast universe as the creation of a Transcendent Being who represents the other reality that we envision in order to become the one true Reality that we know and experience.

Beyond our reason and our powers of logic, beyond the workings of our mind and our ability to articulate our thoughts through words, beyond all the hopes, desires, and emotions that we can make known through language, beyond all that we know and all that we think we know about ourselves and the world, lies the image of the self. This image of our true center would remain forever hidden within the depths of our being if it were not for the possibility of a language of the self that emerges from within us to become the fullest expression of our spiritual identity. Without the image of the self and the appropriate language to make that self known, the true value of humanity and its ultimate worth in the eyes of God would never be made manifest and become known.

What then is the appropriate medium for this inner language of the self? Is it the human body with its sublime message of wisdom, its intelligent design, and its statuesque sculpture of an inward reality? Is it the human intelligence that shines with the luminosity of a mind that translates its thoughts and impressions into a multitude of aspirations and desires? Is it human free will that permits the mind to negotiate its way through a vast range of choices and establish the patterns of behavior that provide the texture of a life? Is it a body of knowledge, such as traditional religion or modern science that condenses and summarizes a complete belief system into an operative worldview?

Through the inner activity across the broad spectrum of the higher human faculties, the outer person becomes manifest and makes itself known as a rational, reflective, and spiritual being dealing effectively with the contingencies of this world. This amounts to expressing the full range of the self in terms of reason, intelligence, heart, imagination, emotions, higher sentiments and the final outcome in the perennial battle of the soul. It is knowledge expressed as wisdom; wisdom expressed through character; character expressed through human behavior; and behavior that is sanctified through the qualifying virtues. It is faith expressed as a knowledge and virtue expressed as the consequence of the free will in view of the Supreme Will of God. It is a knowledge that produces faith, together with an intelligence that produces virtue; for without these four elements, there can be no language of the self and no final fulfillment as a finished, completed, and perfected human being.

We live in a mysterious world that does not fully explain itself. We occupy a time and a place that seemingly lies between two eternities. Nevertheless, through some unfathomable benediction beyond the known self, we have the power to create a life both within and beyond ourselves, to transfigure the image of the self, and to transcend a world not of our making into a world that we ourselves have created, given meaning to, and lived. There is an element of mystery to human origins and there is an element of the secret behind the true nature of the universe that we may never fully fathom; but there must also be a revelatory source of knowledge to enlighten the dark mysteries that surround us and there must be a corresponding means of perfection as the true path to fulfillment.

Through the blessing of the higher spiritual faculties and their modes of knowing and perception, humanity has the capacity to lift the veil that obscures the hidden face of Truth from direct perception. Through the visionary insight of its mind, heart, and soul, it will see, as St. Paul says, "not through a glass, darkly, but face to face" (1 Corinthians 13:12). This final revelation will disclose the first Origin and final End of individual and collective humanity, not in the "warm little pool" of its primal beginnings and some lonely passing into dust and oblivion, but rather in the transcendent knowledge of the one Reality and in the hallowed presence of the Supreme Being.

Epilogue

♣

The Loss and Discovery
of a Hidden Treasure

We have made reference throughout the course of this work to three generic types of human being who represent three key stages of development in the human narrative. We identified them as the primordial couple, followed by traditional believers living in a well-established religious and spiritual environment, and finally the modern individual we are all familiar with living in today's secular, fast-paced world.

We know very little about the primordial first couple Adam and Eve, except what the spiritual traditions have related to us in scripture and through primal feelings empowered by inner spiritual instincts. Still, the symbol of the primordial couple remains within the depths of our being as an echo from some remote past, a potential spark of purity and perfection that lies within, and a premonition of future possibility. The mentality of people who represent a more traditional era will always portray the symbolic image of a believer who rejects the concept of the world as an end in itself and the human being as the sole arbiter of the truth. The traditional person could be identified as *Homo spiritualis*, a numinous soul and a seeker after truth whose vocation is to live life nobly as a spiritual being enclosed within the abode of the body. The modern individual we know intimately: he or she lives within our depths as a creature of our time and as a representative of this place. The shadow of *Homo modernus* casts an image of self that is identified through a faith in the lasting value of this world and in the significance of a phenomenal world whose outward form signifies no inward reality.

The same impulse that drove all our other works has inspired this book as well, namely the desire to question the foundation upon which we build our lives, to answer the call of the inward reality, to explore the meaning of the higher self, and to transcend the limitations of the human condition. In keeping with this effort, we commenced these reflections with some thoughts on the higher human faculties, including cognitive reasoning, luminous intelligence, and the centrality of the heart as the organ of synthesis uniting human intelligence and higher emotions as a votive offering to God.

We then explored the various modes of perception available to the human mind, including spiritual imagination, sacred emotions, and higher sentiments. We went on to consider their effect and significance within the context of the human soul as the battlefield within which the contending forces of good and evil, light and darkness, perfection and imperfection, knowledge and ignorance, wage a perennial war to take possession of and claim sovereignty over the inmost center of every individual within the earthly sphere. Finally, we discussed the forces of spirituality and their consequences, including faith in the absolute knowledge of a Divine Being and the free will to choose the Sovereign Good over a life-time pursuit of self-indulgent choices and a terminal end.

In light of the reams of theory and speculation in all the various fields of science concerning the true nature of life on earth, including its origin, meaning, significance and ultimate purpose, we wanted to thoroughly explore and clearly state an alternative view to the driving force of the worldview proposed by modern science, with its emphasis on the objectivity of the world and its determining physicality. That the universe is the living manifestation of an Absolute Being and that we are the human expression of a divine inspiration are concepts that are unacceptable to the modern mentality, steeped as it is in the closed system of modern science with its insistence on natural causes for the existence of a purely physical world. We might have asked at some point in the narrative why this attitude has come to dominate over the modern psyche if we did not know better than to question the ways of providence. Typical modern-day savants are not in the habit of asking why and look askance at any reference that lies beyond what they consider to be the allegedly objective world of the human senses and the physical matter that modern science perceives by empirical means to be objective, although what it is that actually lends this objectifying quality to either the senses or matter is anyone's guess.

This work has dealt almost exclusively with the inner realm of the mind and the language of the self, outlining a sacred science of knowing and perceiving that virtually defines who we are and what we need to accomplish within the human setting and framework. We have contended that our inner world consists of a borderland that recalls the Quranic reference to the isthmus (*barzakh*) that separates the two seas, a borderland that provides ample room for us to maneuver in our exploration of self, and that bridges the gap between the external world we must deal with every day and the inner world of the spirit that animates our being and gives us our distinctive edge in the kingdom of this world.

The inner world of humanity is a spiritual wilderness of incredible possibility that we inhabit without the need for any formal borders. In it we move freely and easily between the two worlds that shape our existence according to the physical impulses and spiritual instincts that drive us forward in our pursuit of the undivided self. It is within the borderland of the mind and spirit that we commence our search for the sounding cord of our being, a harmonious balance that has the power to return us to our primordial origins, recapture the perfection that we have lost, and become a "finished" person once again, complete and at one with God.

All of the spiritual traditions allude to something that has become hidden or lost as part of the legacy of Adamic man within the primordial tradition. We recall the *soma* of the Hindus and the Persian *haoma*, which refers to the "draught of immortality" that confers on those who receive it the sense of eternity. The origin and purpose of the Sphinx, whose wisdom is summarized in its noble head and whose strength is contained within its leonine body, is enclosed within the folds of some remote epoch as an enduring mystery, a hint of something remote and a premonition of a secret that evanesces into thin air the moment we draw near. The Greeks recount the mythological tale of Jason in search of the Golden Fleece, while in Christianity there is the quest for the Holy Grail, revered as the sacred chalice that contained the blood of Christ and thus the "draught of immortality." The Jews highlight the symbolism of the word in which the true pronunciation of the divine Name has been lost because it could never be uttered. In this respect, we could also refer to the "lost word" of the Masons that symbolizes the hidden secrets of true initiation or the lost word of many of the former revelations whose original texts have disappeared with the lost civilizations of ancient history.

No one from former, more traditional times could have predicted the lost world of the self that is clearly the modern human condition, a condition in which consciousness of a spiritual center has become weakened and the direct connection with the Supreme Center has been lost. In today's world, in what we proudly refer to as the modern world, with all of its sophisticated achievements and technological wizardry, the central pin has been pulled from the axis of the cosmic universe. The vast world of the spirit that we cannot see, touch, or experience with the external senses is lost to us because we have closed the inner eye that once had the power not to see physically, but to experience the metaphysical reality as an inner, human revelation.

Our moral life has disintegrated and has threatened the virtues with extinction. Our intellectual life has been narrowed by the abandonment of ancient customs and traditional beliefs. The profound certainty of our inmost instincts has lost its edge and as a result we are floundering in a sea of doubt and incertitude. We have no picture of ourselves that can confirm our true identity and sustain us through life as a true image of the self. Without the search for the Holy Grail and without the instinctive yearning for the "draught of immortality" that lies within us as a sacred remembrance, we are nobody and we are worth nothing. The physical being that we have come to glorify can be reduced to a single cell rendering us no more glamorous than a period on a page or a bundle of subatomic particles too small to behold, so that we can only see ourselves now "through a glass, darkly" as it were, without the aid of Heaven.

That which speaks to us from within, the imagination that leads us beyond the limitations of the individual self, the intuitive knowledge that seizes the mind with its clear insight and its profound certainty, the higher sentiment that says this is the way my heart is, all of that and more is lost to the modern sensibility with its focus on the material, the physical, and the merely practical. As products of the unique modernist vision, we reach deep down into the world of matter to examine the minutest particles of quantum physics and explore with high-tech space telescopes the vast reaches of the universe in search of a knowledge that will prove our theories right. We wait to be chosen, expecting to hear the secrets of the universe without truly endeavoring to listen, and we want to be called, hoping to see a visionary world of truth and reality without any intuitive insight to substantiate such a sublime vision.

The call of the world and the call of the Spirit are the two halves of a single truth that cannot find their truest expression as isolated parts separated from the Whole. The open gate of the inner faculties, the feeling of expectation, of a hidden inner voice, of promises to be fulfilled and hopes to be realized are all there, in a well-preserved niche within our consciousness, which we preserve as the expression of our inmost selves. It is our higher faculties that receive the essential knowledge of God and perceive the meaning of the one Reality in order to create an external life that reflects the inner person who lives it. The passing of days, the change of seasons, the success of people, the construction of all the churches, temples, and mosques across the earth, the accumulation of friends, money, and fame are one and the same within the context of the world. They happen, they have their place, and then they crumble and are forgotten.

From first origin to final end and from the periphery of this world to the primordial point, the full range of human experience lies in God's hands and remains God's prerogative. Plants and animals experience the gift of life within certain limits, but they do not know God. Humans share the life of the senses with all animals and the experience of the body with minerals and plants. They have other qualities and faculties, however, that they do not share with anyone else, namely an intelligence that can envision the Supreme Intelligence and a consciousness that can respond to the lure of the Absolute and know the Divinity. The more we fail to attune ourselves to the knowledge of God and His unique Reality, the more we begin to think we can live a life that is sufficient unto itself and without the aid of Heaven. The more we fail to recognize, indeed, the more we actively deny, the forms of the eternal wisdom that are embedded within revelation, within the world of nature, and within the human being, the more we confine ourselves to the intellectual, the psychological, and sentient modes of perception, and the more we become the victims of our fragmented intelligence, our fanciful imagination, our unstable emotions, and a subjective, relative perception of what is right and wrong, true and false, illusory and real.

We have written this book for the modern mentality within each of us. We need to transform ourselves once again into the spiritual beings that we are in principle and that we are destined to become in truth. People of this post-modern age live in the world as if they will live here forever, without realizing that the very world for which they live will terminate their lives and forget them. The modern psyche needs to abandon the phantom spirit of this world and recapture the world of the abiding Spirit in which all things are possible and where all mystery is resolved. It is a borderland of the spirit in which the intellect receives a higher knowledge and intelligence sends forth its light, a world in which reason casts a shadow, and the human heart burns with the emotions of higher sentiment. This rarefied borderland contains the source material for the broad range of higher conscious experience. It makes use of spiritual imagination as the search instrument of the soul, and endeavors through its perceptions and insights to expand the horizons of the mind in its perennial quest to internalize the essential knowledge of God.

The human experiment will ultimately earn its rightful place in the cosmic design. The wisdom associated with the name *Homo sapiens* will finally reveal that we are not alone, that there is meaning in holy intimacy, that we can live according to our given nature, and that the truth we have always searched for has finally made itself felt as the supreme awareness of the one Reality. The higher faculties of knowing and perception fulfill their true destiny by becoming reunited once again with the vision of the One God.

The power of the human mind and the very apex of its achievement lies in its ability to build vast kingdoms and sacred sanctuaries and mirages of hope. From a cloudland of our own making, we create an inner world of thinking, imagining, and desiring that will ultimately find a way across the threshold of a greater world that once existed as an ancient, hidden treasure and that now lies in wait of discovery as the seed ground of an eternal life.

Biographical Note

♣

JOHN HERLIHY was born into an Irish-American family in Boston, Massachusetts. Upon completion of his studies at a Paulist seminary, he went in search of adventure as a traveler and teacher and has since worked as a lecturer in English in several Near and Far Eastern countries. In the early 1970s, he made the acquaintance of a Kashmiri Indian whom he now fondly remembers as "the laughing Sufi." In his book *The Seeker and the Way* he explains that his conversion was a raw and unexpected awakening that pulled him back from the abyss and set for him a new direction in coming to terms with the purpose and meaning of his life. Twenty years after his conversion and with a life-long interest in writing, he began to explore through words the complex nature of his relationship with this and the "other" world. In addition to writing for such traditional journals as *Sacred Web* and *Sophia,* his publications include *In Search of the Truth, Veils and Keys to Enlightenment, Modern Man at the Crossroads,* and *Near and Distant Horizons,* all of which reflect upon the disparity between modernity and tradition and the pursuit of spirituality in today's anti-spiritual world.

Index

♣

Index

Index

For a glossary of all key foreign words used in books published by World Wisdom, including metaphysical terms in English, consult:
www.DictionaryofSpiritualTerms.com.
This on-line Dictionary of Spiritual Terms provides extensive definitions, examples and related terms in other languages.

Titles in The Perennial Philosophy Series by World Wisdom

The Betrayal of Tradition: Essays on the Spiritual Crisis of Modernity, edited by
Harry Oldmeadow, 2005

Borderlands of the Spirit: Reflections on a Sacred Science of Mind
by John Herlihy, 2005

A Buddhist Spectrum by Marco Pallis, 2003

The Essential Ananda K. Coomaraswamy,
edited by Rama P. Coomaraswamy, 2004

*The Essential Titus Burckhardt: Reflections on Sacred Art, Faiths, and
Civilizations*, edited by William Stoddart, 2003

Every Branch in Me: Essays on the Meaning of Man,
edited by Barry McDonald, 2002

*Islam, Fundamentalism, and the Betrayal of Tradition: Essays by Western Muslim
Scholars*, edited by Joseph E. B. Lumbard, 2004

*Journeys East: 20th Century Western Encounters with Eastern Religious
Traditions* by Harry Oldmeadow, 2004

Living in Amida's Universal Vow: Essays in Shin Buddhism,
edited by Alfred Bloom, 2004

Paths to the Heart: Sufism and the Christian East,
edited by James S. Cutsinger, 2002

Returning to the Essential: Selected Writings of Jean Biès,
translated by Deborah Weiss-Dutilh, 2004

Science and the Myth of Progress, edited by Mehrdad M. Zarandi, 2003

Seeing God Everywhere: Essays on Nature and the Sacred,
edited by Barry McDonald, 2003

Singing the Way: Insights in Poetry and Spiritual Transformation
by Patrick Laude, 2005

Ye Shall Know the Truth: Christianity and the Perennial Philosophy,
edited by Mateus Soares de Azevedo, 2005